I0824372

MADOO

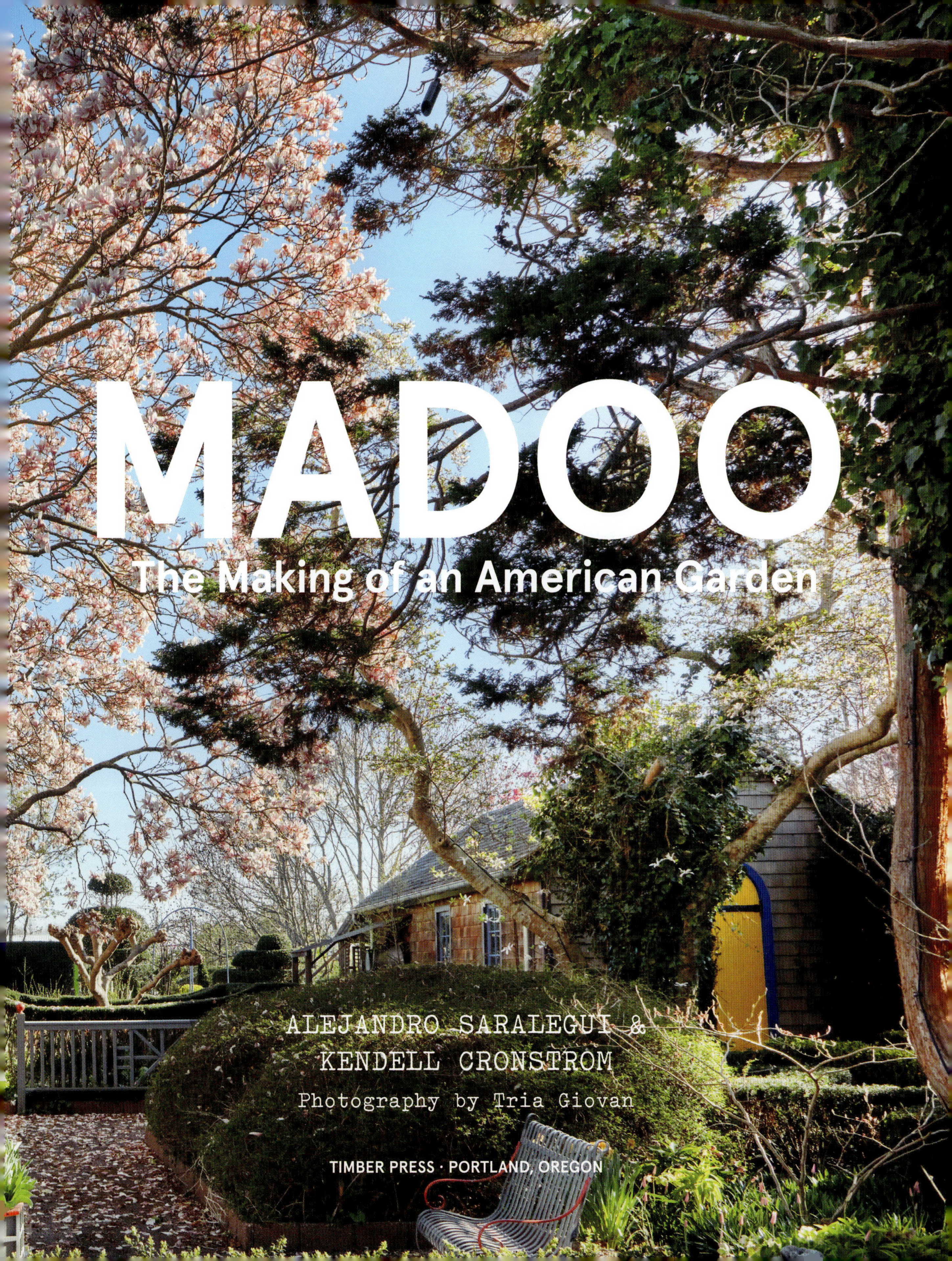

MADOO

The Making of an American Garden

ALEJANDRO SARALEGUI &
KENDELL CRONSTROM
Photography by Tria Giovan

TIMBER PRESS · PORTLAND, OREGON

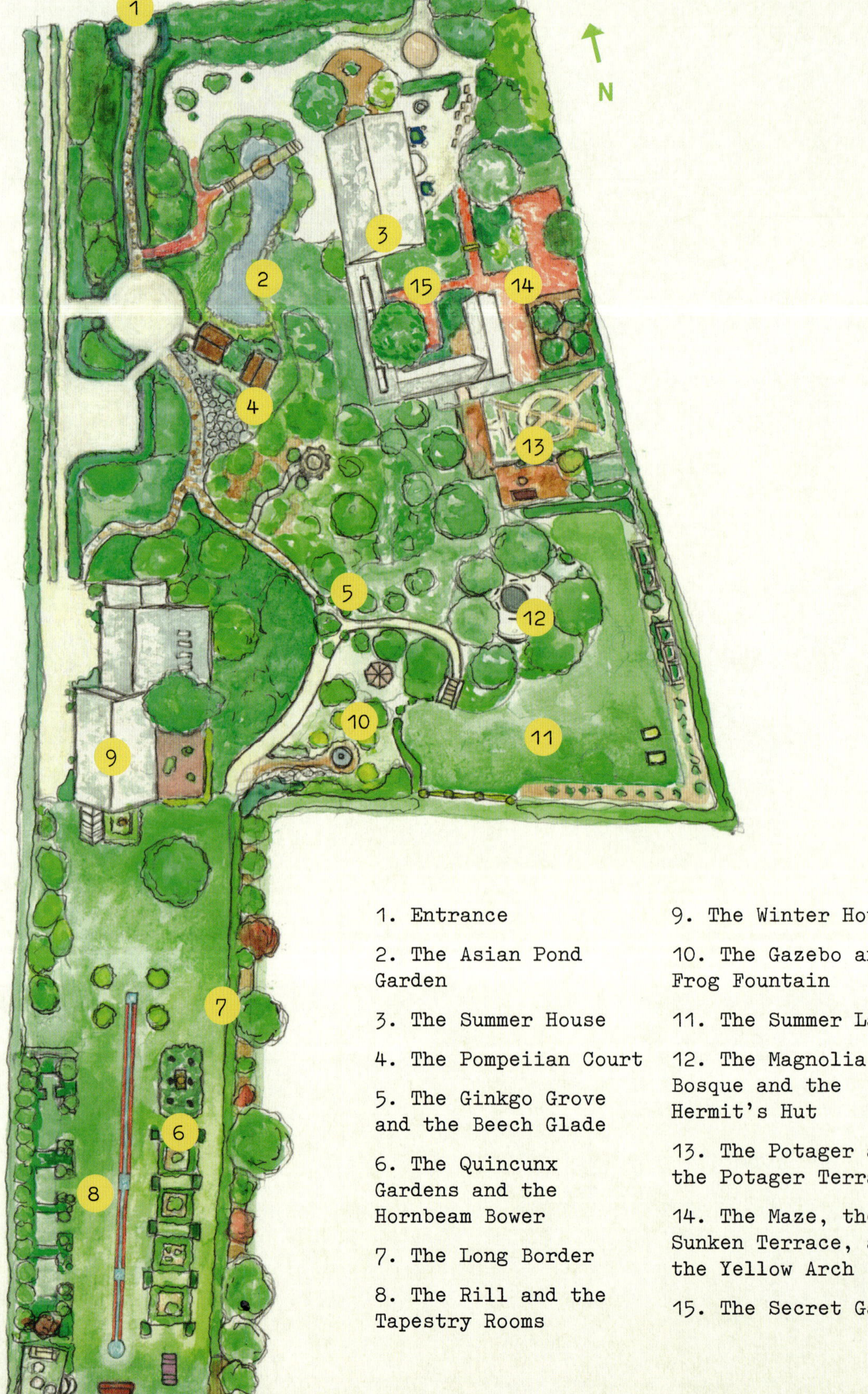
N
1
2
3
4
5
6
7
8
9
10
11
12
13
14
15
1. Entrance
2. The Asian Pond Garden
3. The Summer House
4. The Pompeiian Court
5. The Ginkgo Grove and the Beech Glade
6. The Quincunx Gardens and the Hornbeam Bower
7. The Long Border
8. The Rill and the Tapestry Rooms
9. The Winter House
10. The Gazebo and the Frog Fountain
11. The Summer Lawn
12. The Magnolia Bosque and the Hermit's Hut
13. The Potager and the Potager Terrace
14. The Maze, the Sunken Terrace, and the Yellow Arch
15. The Secret Garden

Contents

MADOO SAGGAPONNACK N Y 11962

May of 1965 found me in a car with the late Realtor Judge Harold Hallock, feeling down and daunted. Nothing at all seemed suitable. But then--

"What is that?"

"Oh, just an old barn. You don't want that. Falling down. It's been on the market for the longest time."

"But I do."

"Do you want to see it?"

"No need. It winked at me."

What I had seen was the roofline of an eighteenth-century hay barn sailing above a hedgerow, in from Main Street in Sagaponack.

"It's on an acre. Some outbuildings, too. All really old. You might get another acre."

A year later, it was mine. In 1967, I moved in and began making the garden I call Madoo.

--Robert Dash

Foreword

OPPOSITE
Seen from across the Asian Pond Garden, guests gather in the Summer Studio at the opening of an August 2024 exhibition by the photographer Michael Light. [Credit: Meagan Ouderkirk]

RIGHT
Fritillaria imperialis 'Early Fantasy'

For more than thirty years, the Madoo Conservancy has been an integral part of the creative community on Long Island's East End, extending a warm welcome through educational and cultural activities, art exhibitions, dance performances, children's programs, and Much Ado About Madoo, its annual summer market and garden party. Madoo not only inspires neighbors and visitors with the beauty that thrives within its hedges, but also guides them to make the all-important connection between gardening, art, and poetry.

As the stewards of Madoo, we have the responsibility of maintaining the masterpiece that Robert Dash created, keeping in mind that he was always imploring us to look toward the future at the same time. As gardeners, we are obliged to be a part of the national botanical preservation narrative, while simultaneously providing visitors with a peaceful and bucolic setting for exploration and discovery.

When Bob came across this dusty patch that "winked at" him in 1965, a horticultural blank canvas presented itself, offering him a new form of artistic expression. Through his extraordinary imagination, his indomitable spirit and idiosyncratic approach to the land, and his kindness and generosity, he left us with a 2-acre treasure to embrace, maintain, and preserve. Doing so is a slow process, the collective effort of gardeners, historians, and local residents whose interest in and concern for science, design, and ecology serve the wide-reaching goals of the gardening community at large. Nearly fifteen years after his death, we still sometimes find ourselves asking, "What would Bob do?" while remembering, always, to look toward the future. Contemplative, sensual, enlightening, and emotional, gardens like Madoo are an art form. They stir something in us and at their best are an integral part of our culture—living, breathing, and looking to us to make the most of them today while ensuring their tomorrows.

—Charlotte Moss

Charlotte Moss is a Madoo Conservancy board member and an interior designer based in New York City and East Hampton, New York, and Charlottesville, Virginia.

Introduction

On the day I was approached about becoming the new director of the Madoo Conservancy in Sagaponack, New York, I was an employee at Broadview Gardens on Town Line Road in the nearby hamlet of Wainscott. I had worked at the bespoke nursery for several years, principally when it was known as Toppings Greenhouse and owned by James Topping, whose family had been landowners in the Hamptons for four centuries. Claudia Thomas, a former fashion executive who was a Madoo board member at the time, pulled me aside and quietly inquired whether I might be interested in the position. Apparently, Madoo's current director wasn't working out and she had thought of me, saying that I knew enough about gardening and all the important local players, too. I said sure, I'd go in for an interview, without thinking much more of it. But Claudia had changed my life forever.

Bob Dash and I had met previously, occasionally at Madoo's gardening lectures in the wintertime or when he stopped by Toppings to look at plants. When we got together to discuss the directorship, our conversation essentially ended with him saying, "Can you start on September 1?" It was 2009, and Madoo was already more than forty years old.

The effects of the Great Recession were everywhere, even in the ivory tower of our tony resort locale, but it didn't matter to Bob: A child of the Depression, he was most comfortable with a simple, even spartan, lifestyle. A born conversationalist with a great wit, he had an amazing ability to make even the most mundane subjects sound both grand and funny, as if from a 1930s talkie. Recounting a humorous encounter from a trip to Italy, he'd say, "Once, on the Ponte Vecchio, a woman frantically asked me if I spoke English, and I responded 'No!'" And he could do a wicked impersonation of Truman Capote, who once lived nearby. Bob

OPPOSITE
Robert Dash, *Sagg Main (#10)* (2007; oil and charcoal on linen, 70 x 60 inches). An abstracted view of Sagg Main Street, where Madoo is located. [Credit: Gary J. Mamay]

TOP
In this undated photograph, Dash sits in the meadow that would eventually evolve into Madoo. The 1850 barn behind him later became the Winter House, where he lived half the year. [Credit: John Reed]

BOTTOM (AND BACKGROUND OF PAGES 6–7)
Madoo, a 1971 acrylic on linen work, depicts Madoo as Dash found it in 1965, but without the 1850 barn that now serves as the Winter House. [Credit: Gary J. Mamay]

ABOVE
Robert Dash, *Wayside Catalog Cover* (1969; acrylic on linen, 60 x 60 inches). Dash painted this landscape using the Wayside Gardens plant and bulb catalog as a model. [Credit: Gary J. Mamay]

didn't suffer fools gladly and had a reputation for being acerbic, but there was never any doubt that he could also be charming, captivating, and gracious.

After I had become established in my new position, friends often asked me how things were going, implying that Bob might be a bit much to work with. Truth be told, we got along well, and he was very fond of my partner (and coauthor of this book), Kendell Cronstrom. He was also extraordinarily intelligent and well-read. Both houses at Madoo have libraries exhibiting his wide range of interests, perhaps spawned while he was being homeschooled as a child due to an illness, although he eventually graduated with honors from Erasmus Hall High School in Brooklyn in 1949. (Bob was also a talented pianist, once telling me that he bailed from a performance at Carnegie Hall due to a case of stage fright.)

After attending college at the University of New Mexico in Albuquerque, where he studied English literature and anthropology, he returned to New York City and fell in with the 1950s demimonde, writing poetry and art criticism and becoming friends with art world up-and-comers like Willem de Kooning, Alex Katz, and Fairfield Porter and poets including James Schuyler, Frank O'Hara, and John Ashbery. By the end of the decade, he had taken up the brush himself, learning at the side of Katz.

His first works in black and white were Abstract Expressionist canvases, although as early as 1961 he had moved on to realism, enjoying his first solo exhibition at the Barone Gallery. On view: a series of landscapes in muted greens, some with subtle architecture incorporated. Soon his works became more colorful, although with a slight melancholy to

RIGHT
The oldest part of Madoo's planted acreage is the Secret Garden (Dash called it the Inner Garden), depicted here circa 1990. [Credit: Karen Balogh]

BELOW RIGHT
Sagaponack neighbor Pingree Louchheim took this photograph in June 1993, just a few years after the Asian Bridge was constructed. Already, it was seamlessly fitting in, vegetation all around it. [Credit: Pingree Louchheim]

LEFT
Bordered on both sides with *Aegopodium podagraria* (foreground) and *Stephanandra incisa* (background), this Dash-designed path leads to the Madoo Conservancy's office. [Credit: Timothy Heslop]

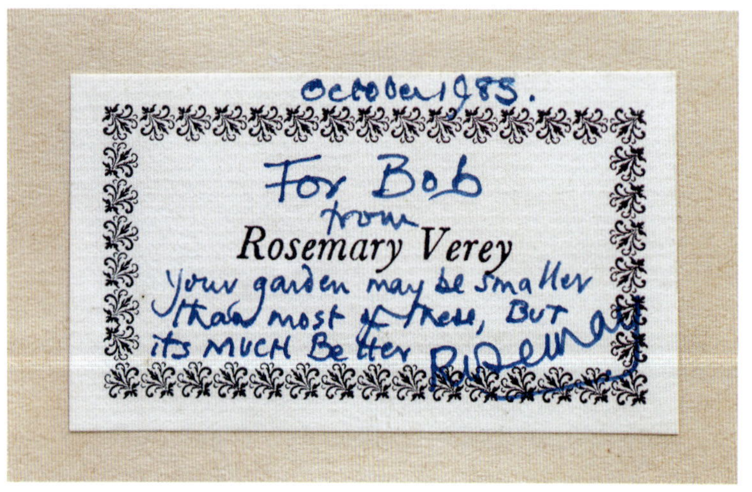

ABOVE
A bookplate attached to John Leyland's *Gardens Old and New,* a gift from Rosemary Verey to Dash, reads, "Your garden may be smaller than most of these, but it is much better. Rosemary." [Credit: Gary J. Mamay]

them and a sort of wartime cast. Reds turned to burgundies, pinks and lavenders to mauves, and blues to hazy grays. He was creating pictorially complex images partly spurred by his imagination but also usually based on a photograph he had taken. (He is said to have painted with a photograph of the day's subject at the end of a long stick held in one hand and a brush in the other.) The image was paramount, and no detail was too small to ignore or wipe away.

In the art world, Bob ultimately carved his own path, although Fairfield Porter's influence is too great to ignore. In the early 1960s, Bob spent a lot of time with Fairfield and Anne Porter at their house on South Main Street in Southampton, and his renderings of domestic bliss can be traced directly to the elder artist. In his landscapes, Bob found a lyrical quality in the quotidian. Telephone poles and wires became graceful lines across a canvas, and the white stripes marking a country lane led the eye with purpose to the greater surroundings of the natural world.

The simple country life suited Bob, but when he moved full-time to the East End at the age of thirty-six, he didn't realize that gardening was to become all-consuming. He had tended a garden at his family's weekend house in Tuxedo Park, in upstate New York, while he was growing up, and it didn't hurt that his mother had a green thumb and never saw a dying plant she couldn't rescue. But in the 1970s, gardening was at best a hobbyist's pursuit or the purview of landscape architects, and no one was really making American gardens—certainly not with a capital G.

At Madoo, Bob continued to paint but also found himself at work on a canvas of a different sort. At first, he made just simple, usually necessary changes to the land, but soon seed and bulb catalogs from specialist nurseries started arriving at the post office and piling up on his dining table. Experiments were made often, either triumphant or quickly abandoned; part-time gardeners were eventually hired to help him tend the rough sketch that would become his masterpiece. People with grander gardens tucked behind the Hamptons' hedgerows suddenly began to take note of what the artist in Sagaponack was up to.

Bob still looms large at Madoo. His learnedness is abundant: Consider the Rill, based on ancient Indo-Persian forebears; the Hermit's Hut, an homage to a quintessential eighteenth-century English folly; and the Secret Garden, drawing on conceits rooted in Italian Renaissance gardens. But his personality is there too. Accommodation for the visitor is seldom considered: Shrubs and plants spilling into paths were not to be admonished, but rather encouraged, since people can just walk around them rather than mar their appearance for the sake of exigency. And flowers were never to be cut for a vase. As with his paintings, Bob was creating memorable images with his exuberant plantings. Green,

LEFT TO RIGHT
The Frog Fountain seen in high summer

A "poetry pot" designed for Seibert & Rice, inscribed with one of Dash's poems, marks the center of Madoo's former entrance terrace. The tuteur protecting the 'Anna's Red' hellebores and other springtime ephemerals is made of branches from the contorted mulberry trees (*Morus alba* 'Unryu') in the Maze. [Credit: Timothy Heslop]

so important in his early canvases, still binds Madoo together, in all its hues and textures.

Bob's last show, mounted posthumously, was an exhibit of pastels, "Blue Hill," at East Hampton's Drawing Room Gallery. I recall him creating these in his studio, Rachmaninoff blaring on a CD player while he pushed his palette table around the room and added marks here and there until forms appeared on each work on paper, one by one. (I made the mistake of interrupting him once and received a withering glare in return.) He had been diagnosed with severe kidney disease and ordered to stop drinking, and as a result, there was a certain joy in these new pieces. Alcohol, which had become his demon, was now banished, freeing Bob to work again, to see friends, to light up his eyes. The pastels evoke Blue Hill, Maine—he had gone there as a young man to paint with Katz—and are a perfect expression of this late-life reawakening.

During his last summer, mostly comprising thrice-weekly dialysis treatments and frequent stays at the hospital, Bob was reading Epicurus's *On Nature* while I was reading Stephen Greenblatt's *The Swerve*; the latter revisits Lucretius's poem "On the Nature of Things," which is about the Epicurean doctrine. The coincidence was not lost on either of us. In August 2013, a few weeks before he died, Bob was scheduled to meet with the curators of the Parrish Art Museum in Water Mill to discuss a donation of his works. When I went into his bedroom to remind him of the appointment, he demurred. "You are Madoo now," he said.

—Alejandro Saralegui

Alejandro Saralegui is the executive director of the Madoo Conservancy in Sagaponack, New York.

CHAPTER ONE

The Beginning

'Crown Princess Margareta', a climber with apricot blooms, has a delicious tea fragrance that permeates the entranceway.

"Magical" is the word visitors use most often when asked for their impressions of Madoo—so much so that it could be a tagline for this sixty-year-old garden located on a scant 2 acres on the eastern end of Long Island. But perhaps not the magical fairy garden that Robert Dash, Madoo's founder, once described it as; rather, it's more the kind of place you can get lost in, that surprises you at every turn just when you think you have it all figured out.

So, what makes Madoo so magical? It can certainly be peaceful in an otherworldly way when you are walking among its skinny sky-high ginkgoes or ambling alongside the Rill and its gently bubbling pools. The colorful hardscaping and painted trim on its two principal structures undoubtedly signify an enchanted garden. And the dahlia bed, a riot of color tucked away in a far corner of the potager, beyond the brussels sprouts and asparagus, is decidedly more surprising than a rabbit coming out of a hat.

Even the weeds, special in their own right and perfectly imperfect, might come across as magical. The water might be murky in the pond and dying water lily leaves not yet removed, but that's of no consequence to the frogs happily sunning themselves on the voluminous pads while dragonflies hover above.

In this organic garden, nothing is ever especially precise. The lawns teem with clover and dandelions, which are never eradicated, as they are an early source of nectar for pollinating bees. The hedges come across as a bit untidy, but that's just what gives the garden its romantic panache. And the roses—yes, they're grown without pesticides and chemical fertilizers—look fabulous in bloom and then fade away until their hips start showing. Never mind blackspot—something else will quickly divert a visitor's attention.

When Dash started Madoo, the garden was simple, just a big sky and meadows and nary a tree on the property or seemingly even nearby. From an elevated perch—either the roof above the library or one of the loft bedrooms of the Winter House—you could see the ocean. In this nascent, barely-there garden, Dash would mow random paths and set a chair at the end to read a book and have a drink. Gradually, those paths became more formalized, paved with concrete garden setts or more famously with wooden disks sliced from telephone poles.

The Secret Garden—Dash originally called it the Inner Garden—came first, once he relocated various sheds on the property and reconfigured them to make the Summer House, a long hall doubling as an ersatz breezeway connecting his painting studio to what became his new residence.

The Secret Garden was the place for experiments. Early visitors to Madoo recall extra-tall yellow hollyhocks pushing through the foliage plants to claim their piece of the sun. Recently, we have been trying to revisit this early density, but with a more tropical air (and a nod to Great Dixter), relying on nonhardy plantings and exotic-looking perennials to differentiate it from the past.

ABOVE
Inside the Summer Studio, where Dash's 1971 acrylic on linen *Madoo* hangs above a reversible flip-back wood and cast-iron train depot bench dating from the 1870s. To the left is a work from the artist's *Florilegium* series, painted in 2000. [Credit: Gary J. Mamay]

OPPOSITE
The Summer House in the early 1970s, trimmed in white and set in a field of *Solidago*. The library extension had been added and the barn that was to be the Winter House already relocated. [Credit: Robert Dash]

After the Secret Garden was established, Dash planted one new area at a time. At first, it was thousands of black pines, which he bought for a pittance from the US Forestry Service (he wrote about their sad demise years later in his column for the *East Hampton Star*). A gardener to the core, Dash looked at death as an opportunity. In the last year of his life, he ordered eighty or so new plants from Forest Farm Nursery in Oregon, which were so small they arrived in just a few boxes. It was the sense of hope that mattered. Might this Cedar of Lebanon survive? What's the difference between these three variegated hakonechloas? How will this streaked barberry perform? Well, the barberry wasn't so happy in the part shade where it was moved a few years ago, so back into the sun it will go, with the hope of reviving its spumoni-patterned leaves. Many of that last delivery didn't make it, as plants aren't terribly cosseted at Madoo—it's up to them to persevere. Maybe a zone 8 plant might survive in the protected Secret Garden, since Madoo has evolved from zone 6b to zone 7b, but it's going to have to do it on its own.

Slowly, under Dash's untrained but confident hand, Madoo took shape on its 1.91 acres in the hamlet of Sagaponack, New York—in the heart of the Hamptons, but not the party-hearty Hamptons. Here, neighbors say a friendly hello when they're picking up mail at the post office and tend to congregate at the local beach at the end of a pothole-filled dirt road. Dash eventually had two residences on the land: the aforementioned Summer House—an amalgam of a 1740 barn turned painting studio, his library, and nineteenth-century sheds converted into a kitchen and sleeping quarters—and an 1850 barn that was relocated from the front of the property to the back and christened the Winter House, a sort of 1970s SoHo loft in a farm vernacular vein. Depending on the time of year and the weather, Dash moved house between both. He eventually added a painting studio and office to the latter, tucked into a berm in the fashion of a timeworn potato barn.

MADOO SAGGAPONNACK N Y 11962

But bear with me as I begin my garden in 1967, gardening in earnest on a plot owned, not rented, and with the intention that it will be a sort of lifelong making of garden pictures. Not rooms. I think of exhibitions, not houses.

--R. D.

MADOO SAGGAPONNACK N Y 11962

A good gardener makes small spaces seem large and large extents intimate. Gardeners manipulate light. They sculpt the very air. Do gardeners always make gardens, or is it, at times, the other way around?

--R. D.

OPPOSITE
The entrance to the Summer Studio is flanked by a pair of *caisses de Versailles* planters containing 'Crown Princess Margareta', a David Austin rose. Before the Summer Studio was renovated in 2017, the decades-old wisteria stretched under the structure and popped up inside on the opposite wall. [Credit: Timothy Heslop]

White trim and brown shingles: The look characterized Madoo at the beginning and resembled virtually everything else in late-1960s Sagaponack. But Dash's remodeling of the buildings was probably considered radical, the kind of thing an artist would do with farm buildings that once rightly belonged to a traditional farmhouse on Sagg Main Street, a classic colonial most recently the home of writer Kurt Vonnegut and now owned by his widow, photographer Jill Krementz. The farmhouse is still visible today from the Sunken Terrace, not far from a partial gristmill stone with an "R" on it—likely meant to denote the Rogers family, the farm's original eighteenth-century occupants.

Color started making its way into the garden via a gate that Dash painted "a mad hue" (no specific documentation exists of what exactly it was) to contrast with a nearby flower. When his mood changed, so might the color of a door or a window frame. Soon, color was everywhere on the hardscaping—sometimes bright, sometimes not. Scratch an old post or a piece of molding, and layers of colors peep through, resembling a palimpsest. Although the harsh Hamptons weather has never been kind to painted wood, color continues to be important, even when it's more modest. Browns and bright blues on the buildings play foil to signature combinations, such as purple and lime green on the stile and red and gray on a pair of iron settees in the Sunken Terrace.

"Green is a color," Dash declared, and so the bright red of a 'Dortmund' rose and the yellow of *Solidago* were always secondary. Layers of green are abundant throughout Madoo, where foliage carries the garden design through a panoply of different textures and tones. From the privet hedges at the entrance to mounds of shrubs such as *Stephanandra incisa* and rhododendrons and myriad ground covers, green predominates from the ground to the sky, from the creeping thyme to the leafy boughs of the tallest trees.

As the garden evolved, burgundy-leaved plants and trees caught Dash's

attention—witness the Japanese maple (*Acer palmatum*) in the Long Border or the almost black leaves of a *Cimicifuga* in the Beech Glade. Even the imperious Rosemary Verey left an unexpected yet indelible mark: A dear friend of Dash's, the British garden designer and prolific author is largely credited with the preponderance of yellows at Madoo, particularly the laburnum arbor. (Verey kept a similar, famous arbor at Barnsley House, her home in Gloucestershire.) Golden cypress (*Chamaecyparis pisifera*) standards surrounding the Frog Fountain and a mound of golden cypress outside the Summer House's dining room window are exemplars of Verey's influence.

The self-taught Dash's gardening talent was twofold. He was an endlessly curious plantsman and a designer with a twinkle in his eye, conjuring follies both natural and man-made to delight and amuse. Dotted throughout Madoo's landscape, these follies advance visitors on their explorations of the garden, through tightly compressed and densely planted areas that suddenly open onto vast expanses of lawn. Each structure—from the purple Gazebo to the rose-studded Hermit's Hut—is grounded with plantings that soften their edges and make them seem as if they have been there forever.

Dash often referred to Madoo as a museum of garden design, akin to a three-dimensional book on the subject, but he also cautioned that it isn't preserved in amber. It allows for change, certainly within his lifetime and today as well. Change is at the heart of Madoo, as it continues to engage and awe visitors in new and unexpected ways.

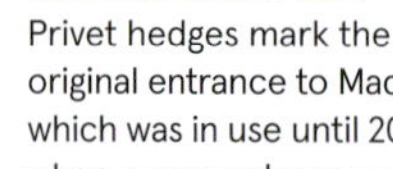

LEFT AND BELOW LEFT

Privet hedges mark the original entrance to Madoo, which was in use until 2025, when a new welcome center opened elsewhere on the property. Three shallow brick steps, flanked by a pair of nineteenth-century Chinese granite foo dogs, led to a terrace where visitors would congregate. On the left, a female dog clutches a pup, and on the right, a roaring male rests his right paw on a pearl. The two late-spring pots are high English country, featuring pink scabiosa, blue lupines, *Cosmos bipinnatus* 'Cupcakes White', *Euphorbia* 'Diamond Frost', and dark blue larkspur, all surrounding a tall fuchsia standard.

BELOW

Planted in the autumn, tumbleweed onion bulbs (*Allium schubertii*) are simply scattered about and left to perform where they land.

OPPOSITE

Astride the Summer Studio, a sweetbay magnolia (*Magnolia virginiana*) is set in a bed of palm sedge (*Carex muskingumensis*) and *Geranium wlassovianum*. After the starlike *Allium schubertii* bloom, they leave tawny sculptural seed heads behind. The defining short hedge of *Lonicera nitida* 'Baggesen's Gold' in the foreground looks good both sheared and left natural.

OPPOSITE

By midsummer, the *Paulownia tomentosa* reaches 10 feet, with more to go. The platter-sized leaves are a result of a yearly autumn stumping, when the entire tree is cut down to its gnarled trunk. In the spring, the gardeners allow one to three shoots to grow to extraordinary heights, drawing energy from a thirty-plus-year-old root system.

BELOW

Dwarf gold variegated bamboo engulfs a wheel-away bench, which Dash crafted using an old wheel he found in the original 1740 barn. The short bamboo needs to be kept in check or planted with a barrier.

RIGHT

The wheel-away bench, today a glossy black, was once painted in Palm Beach pastels, perhaps to match the pink honeysuckle at left. [Credit: Robert Dash]

BELOW RIGHT

A light snowfall accentuates a curvaceous boxwood hedge and, behind it, the white stems of a ghost bramble (*Rubus thibetanus*), situated between mounds of adult ivy and *Ilex × meserveae* 'Blue Princess'. The Victorian-era American cast-iron bench is identical to those once found in the White House Rose Garden. Dash stripped its white paint and left it rusticated to coordinate with the dying late-summer leaves of lily of the valley.

Multiple plantings of *Taxus*, rhododendrons, and a *Fagus sylvatica* 'Purpurea Pendula' shield Madoo's former entrance on the street, giving way to a brick-and-gravel path that leads visitors to the Summer Studio. This gravel garden plays host to myriad self-seeded and potted plants, lending a slightly Provençal air to the space. Madoo's gardeners weed out the *Tanacetum parthenium* 'Aureum' to create a chartreuse petticoat of daisies against the evergreens. The nineteenth-century banded French stone column, a gift, pops out of a mélange of *Agave americana*, flowering and scented pelargoniums, *Iris* × *robusta* 'Gerald Darby', and *Lavandula* × *intermedia* 'Grosso'.

ABOVE
The silken petals of the 'Yellow Purissima' tulip glisten on the Winter House terrace.

OPPOSITE
A *Magnolia* x *soulangeana* looks like a spun-sugar confection against an impossibly clear cerulean sky.

English Bones, American Flesh

by Robert Dash

My garden is at the far eastern end of Long Island, in New York State, in a town settled in 1656. It is set amidst fields continually farmed since that time, and one would need a maul to separate it from its profoundly English influences. Yet it might take a wedge struck with equal force to pry it from its continuous involvement with the patterns of Abstract Expressionism, a largely American form of painting.

Within that pattern much else went toward the making of my garden: a love of Indian paths, rather like the secret walks small children make (which counts a lot for how one moves through my garden); an admiration of the roan beauties of abandoned farmland pierced by red cedars laced and tied by dog roses, honeysuckle, and brown, dry grass; the memory of a meadow of a single species of short, gray-leaved, flat-topped, open-flowered goldenrod, whose October display was feathered by hundreds of monarch butterflies. I have a stubborn Calvinist belief in utility, which causes me to plant vegetables among flowers, use herbs as borders and berry bushes as ornamentals. The brutish littoral climate leads me to choose only such plants as have infinite stamina. There are recollections of an ancestor who planted hollyhocks at the gate and lilacs out back—but all gardens are a form of autobiography. Moreover, as a painter, I am predilected toward shape, mass, and form and have learned that the predominant color of all gardens is green, and all the rest is secondary bedeckment. Finally, there is something else—a fierce addiction to privacy, which is why my windbreak is thicker than it need be.

Madoo, which in an old Scots dialect means "My Dove," is the name of my garden of 1.91 acres, and I have been at it now since 1967. I have gone about it as I would a painting, searching for form rather than prefiguring it, putting it through a process more intuitive than intellectual. The blunders are there to learn from; the successes, more often than not, are the result of bold throws. I started from the house and went out toward the edges, often revising solid achievements until they seemed made of finer matter, like marks and erasures of work on paper, which sometimes may be torn and fitted again in collage.

Although I like white on white (the *Clematis* 'Duchess of Edinburgh' on a white fence over *Rosa* 'Blanc Double de Coubert'), and I like to whiten white by throwing autumn clematis (*C. terniflora*) over yew and *C.* 'Huldine' over holly, the major push is for green on green. I have never cared much for all-gray gardens or all-blue gardens; indeed, I am not certain that they are ever successful, color being too quixotic to control in that fashion, full of lurking betrayals, so that sky blue becomes sea blue or slate blue and then not blue at all. The air over my garden, from whose several points I can see the Atlantic surf, is full of a most peculiar double light, rising and falling, and is itself one of the heroes of my landscape, kinder to foliage and bark than to flowers. Wild air will always do the painting. I have increased the atmosphere's multiple shimmers by putting in three small ponds, above whose surfaces small mists sometimes gather. In contrast I have made darkness with a copse of twisted, pruned arctic willows and another of a spinney of fastigiata ginkgoes, the former underplanted with a mix of *Epimedium*, woodruff, Japanese wood anemones, and ferns, and both washed with the littlest of spring bulbs. Paths are of brick, pebbles, setts, disks of telephone pole, or grass. Curves alternate with strict straight geometries, the better to bound, heighten, and confine the predominantly relaxed, semiwild, superabundant atmosphere I like.

A meadow garden has been quite successful. Formerly, it was lawn giving a rather dull view from the dining table, made duller by summer heat and inevitable drought. America is no climate for lawns. I did not starve the soil to make the meadow but plunged robust, thrusty perennials through the grass into pits carefully nourished with well-rotted manure and much peat moss. It is roughly oval with a backing of Nootka cypress, *Cryptomeria*, and rhododendron, whose darks perfectly outline the brighter foil of foliage.

To my way of seeing, a garden is not a succession of small rooms or little effects but one large tableau, whose elements are inextricably linked to the accomplishment of the entire garden, just as in painting all passages conduce to the effect of the whole. Lack of keyed strength in any one of them may lower the pitch and thrust of the finished canvas.

A muting of a too-perfect area is often in order, no matter how lovely it might be. Just so I have found 'Silver Moon' clematises are too huge a cynosure to be acceptable to the general garden, and I have taken them out. One can very definitely have too much of a good thing, unless it be some grand ground cover like *Lamium* 'Nancy', whose very modest performance excludes it from the egregious. Subtlety is always more alluring. The quieter painting enters the heart and stays, when one of tremendous impact has long since faded away.

I do not paint in the way that I garden or garden as I would employ the brush, although the process is often the same—both are arts of the wrist, the broadest, largest sort of signature, if you will, highly idiosyncratic, the result of much doing, much stumbling, and highly intuited turns and twists before everything fits and adheres to the scale of one's intention. A good tree must often be moved to a more reticent spot when it begins to dominate and thus ruin the total orchestration. Beautiful tunes don't end up as symphonies, nor do witticisms write books. Certain flowers

CLOCKWISE FROM NEAR RIGHT
Dash's own undated photograph of his hat on a gatepost at Madoo [Credit: Robert Dash]

Robert Dash in the Summer Studio, circa 2007, when the walls were painted orange and he was gessoing prints initiated years earlier for new works [Credit: Bärbel Miebach]

Robert Dash, *Rising Water* (1983–84; oil on linen, 50 x 70 inches). In the early years, Dash walked daily with his dog to nearby Sagg Pond, but new construction later prevented access. [Credit: Gary J. Mamay]

may emblazon a room but be abusive to a fine garden. For that reason and that of stamina and the ability to take the brunt of the climate (I am in zone 7a, whose average lowest temperature is five to zero degrees Fahrenheit), I choose older varieties of the plant kingdom, whose foliage and blossom are, more often than not, circumspect and discreet.

I am now becoming more geometric. In front of the Winter House and Winter Studio I have just installed a brick path I call a view-swiper. It is 120 feet long (flying out to the potato fields and to the ocean, bringing all that fine view inside the purview of the garden as if it were mine), 8 feet wide at the near end, 6 at the far, with eighty roses ('Fru Dagmar Hastrup') on the sides. The far border will have other, taller *rugosa* roses and daylilies mixed with teasels. The site is but a narrow spur attached to my property, surrounded by changing crops whose patterns of growth and tilling are overwhelmingly seductive, requiring only the simplest sort of anchor to moor the peninsula.

My canvases now have changed, too, and are rather like foliant form held very close to the eye. Both gestures, then, are new for me, and the feeling from both is a bit scary, akin to that of someone in the middle of a new high-wire act performing over a slowly withdrawing net. The air of gardens and paintings now seems to me to be filled with a

wild, deliciously cold oxygen through which I can still see the first plain view of the working barns I converted three decades ago, gray above a blowing field of grass. That verdure, it seems to me, was the very soul of the place "working backwards, year by year," as John Koethe wrote in "The Near Future," until it "reached the center of a landscape."

The English bones with which I began now seem entirely covered by what I have done, but that is the way of flesh.

Robert Dash (1931–2013) was the founder of Madoo. This essay is taken from his 2000 collection of writings, Notes from Madoo.

CHAPTER TWO

The Asian Pond Garden

As summer begins in earnest, the pond goes green except for the flowering water lilies in its upper and lower levels, where frogs sun themselves on the leaves. Forming a verdant backdrop to the bridge are a multistemmed *Cryptomeria japonica* and a weeping beech (*Fagus sylvatica* 'Pendula'). In mid-May, the fully leafed-out beech forms a magical "doorway" to the garden, a transporting experience.

For at least a decade prior to establishing Madoo, Robert Dash had been working as an artist and counted the likes of Alex Katz and Fairfield Porter among his contemporaries. Early on, as Madoo was beginning to take shape, he built a pond adjacent to the Summer Studio, which he could see while he was painting. Simply dug out of the flat earth and filled with a hose, it became a hive of aquatic life after Dash poured in a jar of mucky water from nearby Sagg Pond: peepers in April and dragonflies in June. A pair of flat bridges, added later, completed the scene.

Virtually any surface was a canvas for Dash, who rendered his new pond on a black-painted Art Deco–era armoire that now stands in the Winter House's dining room. The pond's bridges traverse the armoire's doors amid a swirling eddy of turquoise and light blue water. Riffing on the trademark characteristics of a Coromandel screen, the cabinet suggests Dash's interest in chinoiserie, its multitudinous motifs pervading the garden for years to come.

In the mid-1980s, Dash rebuilt the pond, dividing it into upper and lower levels and installing a new, partially covered bridge across it. Vaguely Asian-inspired, with a gently curving shape and red oval bentwood hoops forming part of its framework, it nods slightly to Monet's bridge at Giverny. A petite metal table and a yellow-painted Lloyd Loom stool sit beneath the pagoda-shaped canopy, providing an exquisite perch for contemplating the water beneath. It was one of Dash's favorite resting spots, framed by a weeping beech that now stands almost three stories tall.

As long as the hose was connected and turned on, the water made a quietly pleasing sound and added to the atmospherics, with droplets glinting in the sun and the trees blurrily reflected on the pond's surface. A rivulet of local stones set in concrete, intended to help hold the pond's rubber liner in place, deteriorated around 2016: The concrete was showing its age, and the pond now required daily refilling to maintain the waterline. Out went the unnatural edging, the cracked liner, and three decades' worth of decomposed leaves that had settled to the bottom and were dispatched to the compost pile.

The latest iteration hews closely to Dash's vision, with the addition of a small waterfall separating the upper and lower levels of the pond. Rocks set on pebbles now weigh down the lining, and a few clumps of *Acorus gramineus* 'Ōgon' were broken up and redistributed to soften the edges and add an element of unity, creating a truly golden pond. At the suggestion of the contractor, a climbing hydrangea was added at the waterfall's edge as a ground cover (or, in this case, a rock cover). The common adage associated with climbing hydrangea, "Year one it sits, year two it grows to knee height, and year three it takes off," has proven true. Arching gracefully next to the waterfall, a mushroom-shaped *Acer palmatum* 'Jiro shidare' serves as a transition point from the taller trees down to the lowest level of the water. In autumn, its leaves turn a mottled orange red, bringing attention to its domed

MADOO SAGGAPONNACK N Y 11962

The Oriental Bridge, having exceeded the budget by an enormous amount, is also known as the Bridge of the Bankrupt Painter. A cherry picker had to be rented to haul the foundation telephone poles. A rather elaborate Rube Goldberg sort of steam oven was fabricated in the Summer Studio to bend and curve the cedar shingles, so necessary for the configuration of an Oriental bridge roof, the tale being that, with this curve, imps, goblins, witches, and other riffraff of the underworld are hard-pressed to gain purchase and instead slide off, screaming imprecations as they go.

--R. D.

shape. The Asian Pond Garden is not, it must be said, a strictly Japanese or Chinese water garden. Dash simply paid homage with the bridge and a selection of Asian trees.

Nothing here references a distant landscape, as in Japanese gardens: There are no scholar's rocks, and the presence of moss is limited. Instead, the whole is a harmonious combination of Dash's interpretation of what an Asian water garden might be. A large *Magnolia* × *soulangeana* stretches against the upper branches of the *Fagus sylvatica* 'Pendula', its springtime flowers perfuming the air. As the blooms die, the pink-and-white petals fall to the ground, blanketing the soil and the pond in a pastel-colored carpet. On the far end of the bridge, a *Cryptomeria japonica* rises in tandem with a cloud-pruned *Ilex glabra*. Two *Stewartia pseudocamellia* grow on either side of the pond's lower level. A third mysteriously snapped at the base a few years ago.

At the southern end of the pond, Madoo's new welcome center (previously the site of the dilapidated Loo building) is covered in *Akebia*

CLOCKWISE FROM NEAR RIGHT

Raking sunlight brightens a snowy afternoon. The steps to the bridge are made of local red cedar, and the square-cut stones are eighteenth-century ship ballast, found during the renovation of the Summer Studio.

Despite freezing temperatures, the golden *Acorus gramineus* 'Ōgon' stays pert, softening the water's rocky edges.

A mound of *Hakonechloa macra* takes on pale straw tones in the winter, contrasting with the evergreen fronds of the 'Brilliance' autumn ferns.

quinata and *Schizophragma hydrangeoides*, offering a passage from the Far East to the local Hamptons farm vernacular. At this edge of the pond, *Petasites japonicus* spreads its large round leaves in the spring, while a Japanese maple with yellow bark and an upright habit forms an exclamation point. The Loo building had comprised three parts: two extant sheds that Dash found on the property and a flat-roofed structure connecting them. As in the past, the exterior of the new structure is decorated with three narrow dressing mirrors from the local general store attached to a cedar wall. The mirrors are infrequently cleaned, as it is less likely that birds will fly into glass speckled with dust and dirt. With their hazy reflections of the *Akebia quinata* that surrounds them, they offer a bit of mystery. At this humble juncture, Dash's skill as a designer becomes evident. Heavy, almost forestlike planting mediates the potential awkwardness of an Asian-inspired water garden immediately adjacent to a colonial-era barn, a composition that is painterly to the core.

Just behind the Asian Pond Garden, a series of curved paths edged in short, thin scrappy boxwood hedges lead from the young Ginkgo Grove to the bridge and the pond's lower level. These remnants from the garden's beginning, now shrouded in the darkness of towering trees, are simply a means of getting from one point to another. Still, sheets of lily of the valley perfume the air in the springtime, ancient clumps of daffodils bloom, and white crocuses push up through dark green liriope, all beating the odds in a woodland of English chestnut, European beech, alders, and oaks.

On the Summer House side of the Asian Pond Garden, *Dryopteris erythrosora* 'Brilliance', chosen for its bronze-toned new fronds, complements the cinnamon-colored bark of a *Stewartia pseudocamellia*.

OPPOSITE

Growing within the pond, *Pontederia cordata* produces spiked purple flowers, edible seeds, and arrow-shaped leaves.

CLOCKWISE FROM TOP LEFT

A *Rhododendron luteum* grows on the far side of the pond, its fragrant yellow blossoms reflected on the water. Also known as the pontic azalea, it's the only azalea native to Europe. [Credit: Alejandro Saralegui]

In early spring, a *Magnolia × soulangeana* unleashes its thick pink-and-white blossoms high above the pond.

Hydrangea anomala subsp. *petiolaris* is planted at the edge of the pond, cushioning the waterfall along with the mushroom-shaped *Acer palmatum* 'Jiro shidare'.

Perennial pink water lilies are not only beautiful but also shade the water, limiting algae growth.

CLOCKWISE FROM NEAR RIGHT

The stewartia's camouflage bark comes to life in the low autumn light.

The stewartia's flowers fall face up, resembling fried eggs on a bed of liriope and sweet woodruff (*Galium odoratum*).

The pondside cedar bench, now about forty years old, looks decrepit but is still quite sturdy. Red berries on the umbrella-pruned *Ilex verticillata* provide a festive accent.

OPPOSITE

A view from beneath the weeping beech and its almost translucent new growth in early June

MADOO SAGGAPONNACK N Y 11962

I make many of my walks out of squares and rectangles of tinted concrete, which sounds awful but isn't. They are locally made and come in red, black, or tan, each hideous in its own colorful way, but fading is mercifully built into them when their pores fill with soil.

--R. D.

OPPOSITE

A large *Pinus strobus* 'Pendula', its needles retained as mulch, separates the old Loo shed from the Summer House. The wooden wheelbarrow, made on-site at Madoo, is painted the same colors as the Summer House.

CLOCKWISE FROM ABOVE

Covered in moss, paths made of red-tinted cement pavers are bordered by boxwood hedges that lead toward the old Loo shed.

The lavender 'Ramona' clematis complements the plummy chocolate and blue trim on the door to the library.

'Brilliance' autumn ferns are cut back in early March when they are looking tatty. In less than a month, new fronds emerge.

From virtually any approach at Madoo, the Asian Pond Garden's bridge is almost obscured until you are up close. The Summer House is to the right, with *Clematis* 'Ramona' and climbing roses flanking the door to the library.

ABOVE
The Asian Pond Garden is reflected in mirrors that hang on the north side of Madoo's brand-new Welcome Center, on the site of the former Loo shed.

OPPOSITE
At pond's edge, the overlapping leaves of *Petasites japonicus* resemble traditional *kumo*, or clouds, found in Japanese drawings, paintings, and ceramics.

As the trees green-up in mid-May, the pond is still quite visible. Soon water lilies will cover its surface and the *Acorus* on the edges will grow to give it a golden ruff.

CHAPTER THREE

The Summer House

The red living room features seating pieces covered in an ikat stripe designed by Madeline Weinrib. A Murano glass vase with bronze mounts, created by Silvia Buscaroli for Seguso Vetri d'Arte in 1985, sits on a barley-twist stand.

In 1971, four years after he moved in at Madoo, Robert Dash painted the Summer House as he had originally found it, relying on memory and perhaps some early snapshots. The view, looking from Sagg Main Street toward the original 1740 barn, includes a few telephone poles and their lyrical wires among a tangled canopy of street trees. The 1940s-style grayed-out palette of sages and rusts and dull lavenders further amplifies the barren landscape. Aside from the crumbling barn building and the fallow farm field beyond, there was virtually nothing here.

In the mid-1960s, Dash had visited the property for the first time with a Realtor. There was still a cow occupying the 1740 barn, which also included a mid-nineteenth-century barn attached to its north side. In his painting, Dash blacked out the wall where the latter structure—eventually detached and destined to become the Winter House—once stood. The 1740 barn remained where it was, transformed into Dash's painting studio and living room. Dash added windows and glass-paned doors, allowing in as much light as possible, along with a boost from fluorescent tubes circumnavigating the room and illuminating the painting area. A third of the barn was earmarked as the living room, entered awkwardly from a tight corner door. Now painted a watermelon-y coral, the walls were originally white—all the better to show off a rotating display of Dash's paintings—and the bulk of the furniture installed during that time still exists today. The double-height rooms presumably accommodated the barn's hayloft, pierced near the top with still-functional window-paned doorways that originally connected the second-floor spaces.

The flow of the "bordello red" living room—as Dash described it after he ditched the white walls during his later, extensive experimentations with color—changed over time. A restoration in 2018 introduced a pair of glass-paned French doors that provide easier access from the painting studio to the living room and the library beyond. Today, the living room is now more of a salon for informal gatherings and dinners for up to thirty people. Now, as before, all Dash paintings on the walls date from different periods of his career to keep the space from becoming static. These range from his early pastels to oversize florals done late in his life.

The wall of mirrors at one end of the room was rehung as he had initially installed it, with the addition of just a few more from his collection, an eclectic mix ranging from proper gilded nineteenth-century frames to tiny dime-store ovals to a contemporary blue glass slab sheathed in a carapace of raw metal. The furnishings in the room have undergone judicious editing. A mix of family furniture and collected pieces, the grouping includes a rare double bentwood rocker facing the picture window overlooking the Secret Garden. There was a small pond for the sitter to admire, but it later developed a leak. Now the ever-changing view includes a spectacular vista of vibrant *Crocosmia* 'Lucifer' against a verdant backdrop of Australian tree ferns and banana plants.

In the late 1960s, Dash connected the barn to a pair of smaller outbuildings that were to

RIGHT
In the early 1970s, when the Atlantic Ocean was still visible from the library's roof, Dash painted this view directly onto a fire screen of Anglo-Indian origin. It's positioned against the library's eastern wall, which is dedicated to gardening books, as it was in Dash's time. The 800 or so volumes range from nineteenth-century tomes on garden design to flower-arranging primers by Constance Spry to titles by Dash's contemporaries. The Madoo Conservancy continues to add to the collection yearly.

OPPOSITE
The dining table at the southern end of the library is surrounded by ladder-back dining chairs that Dash had retained from his early residences in New York City. The lath strips on the renovated ceiling cover HVAC foil, which creates a quiet shimmer. The large oil on linen painting is from Dash's *Fields and Furrows* series of 1998–99. The window trim matches the Dash-mixed color in the red living room.

become sleeping quarters and a kitchen. To join these disparate parts, he built the only modern piece of the puzzle, a corridor-like library featuring a dazzling floor lined in black and creamy yellow cement garden pavers, arranged in a sort of checkerboard pattern. The ceiling insulation was partially covered by strips of wood lath, which lend extra linearity to this especially long space. The insulation's foil backing peeks through the lath, adding shimmer and a lovely reflective quality as sunlight enters from the dining area windows at the room's southern end.

Dash's collection of gardening books grew, and so he added more bookcases to the library, until all the walls were covered floor to ceiling. Heavy wooden doors open outward off the room, so as not to steal precious square footage from the already tight environs, and screen doors are on the inside, designed that way by Dash to take up a smaller footprint while providing cross-ventilation in a structure that hadn't been configured for air-conditioning.

A 1972 Dash canvas depicts his dining room, a space that remains much the same today: an unprepossessing oak table surrounded by ladder-back chairs and a rickety chinoiserie étagère occupying a corner. The only difference in the rendering is a view of the neighboring farm field, a vista now fully obscured by plants that have been growing beyond the window for more than fifty years.

Dash was interested in cooking and kept books by culinary potentates like Diana Kennedy and Craig Claiborne on hand, but the kitchen adjoining the dining room was ascetic, with open shelving, a cheap boxy fridge and electric stove, and a small stainless-steel double sink. Despite its humble accoutrements, this utilitarian space must have seemed like a dream to Dash, who used a Sterno flame to heat his soup during his first summer in residence at Madoo.

Two bedrooms lie beyond the kitchen in an enfilade that doesn't allow much in the way of privacy. Hardly bigger than the full-size bed that sits inside it, Dash's emerald-green bedroom is capped with a peaked roof and sports a feature wall hung with poems encased in plastic box frames. (Written by friends including

MADOO SAGGAPONNACK N Y 11962

Red does rev me up and I enjoy my red living room of a shade pure bordello as much as my guests, although babble frequently results, and serious conversation seems to reign in the dining room which is a wet Tuscan brown.

--R. D.

MADOO SAGGAPONNACK N Y 11962

I move to the Summer House at about the time the apples blossom but this too has no fixed date and is based on nothing more than when that restless malaise called spring fever inevitably strikes hold and I want change. I want to be doing and then I want to loiter. I am at my most animal, wanting to change burrows, to clean, sort, rearrange. Back and forth from Winter to Summer House, pitching and fretting. Away with fust. Down with fuss. New lampshade here, touch of paint there. Pillows. That chair has got to go. That painting goes into the racks and a new one goes up.

--R. D.

OPPOSITE
One of six chairs originally designed by Dash for the Winter House dining area, this rather severe perch now occupies a corner of the Summer Studio, adjacent to the red living room. Dash often used to sit in one of the chairs outside, greeting visitors on open days.

Douglas Crase and James Schuyler, the poems are facsimiles; the original manuscripts were acquired in 2011 by Yale University's Beinecke library.) Spare furnishings and art include a pine armoire, a maple dresser, a prized Willem de Kooning drawing (signed "Bill"), and a charming Alex Katz cutout of a dog.

Dash's bath features terra-cotta pavers on the floor and a homemade vanity inset with an antique Portuguese ceramic bowl used as a sink. Ivory opera scarves hang from a wooden piece of farm equipment repurposed as an ersatz towel rack. The entire enfilade includes a total of seven dressers, some painted the prevailing emerald green and studded with early-twentieth-century floral decals. The kitchen and back bedroom suite feature a unique connective tissue: a bright yellow and blue spatter-dash floor painted by Dash, who was obsessed with spongeware, speckle ware, and old New England craft traditions. The Summer House's library, dining room, kitchen, and bedrooms form a loose C-shaped configuration around the densely planted Secret Garden and its burbling baptismal stoup, with multiple windows and access doors embracing the view. As with virtually everything, Dash was always thinking about his garden.

Little is known about the double bentwood rocker that has faced the low picture window and its mesmerizing view of the Secret Garden since the 1970s. Mirrors collected by Dash hang on the far wall. To the left is Dash's 1972 rendering of the dining area; at far right, a vintage apothecary vase occupies a table.

SPIRIT OF PLACE
ART
HAUTE BOHEMIANS GREECE

CLOCKWISE FROM RIGHT
Outside the door to the library, a large double-file viburnum (*Viburnum plicatum*) is underplanted with the native *Gillenia trifoliata*, which produces an explosion of white flowers in the late spring.

A detail of the doublefile viburnum outside the library

An orange honeysuckle (*Lonicera* × 'Mandarin') climbs a trellis outside a dining room window.

OPPOSITE
At one end of the library, a drafting desk is paired with a paint-splattered wooden stool from the Summer Studio. The wall's wood siding is original to the 1740 barn.

BELOW

The kitchen opens to Dash's bedroom, where a wall is hung with facsimiles of poems by friends including James Schuyler, Douglas Crase, Frank O'Hara, and more. (The originals were acquired by Yale University's Beinecke library in 2011.) The hardy *Begonia grandis* grows in the adjacent Secret Garden.

OPPOSITE, FROM TOP

The nineteenth-century French boudoir wicker chair on the spatter-dash floor is painted the same green as the walls in Dash's steeply peaked bedroom.

Dash's guests used this hybrid bathroom/dressing room, also painted green and featuring a spatter-dash floor. Photos of friends and family dating back to the early twentieth century sit atop the taller dresser; the monoprint above the three-drawer bureau is by Claudia Thomas, a former Madoo Conservancy board member.

BELOW
A 1972 tondo by Dash, depicting Madoo with white trim and the garden virtually all meadow, hangs in the guest room. The fringed green bedspread is Moroccan.

RIGHT COLUMN, FROM TOP
A 1962 pastel—rendered on vintage French rag paper acquired from the Metropolitan Museum of Art—rests on a wicker hamper in the guest room. A pair of antique mahogany canoe paddles sit astride the ceiling beams.

A path made of bluestone and broken bits of red concrete pavers was laid in 2017 alongside the northern end of the Summer House and Studio complex.

OPPOSITE
Dash's bathroom has a floor of varnished garden pavers. Silk opera scarves hang from a rustic piece of painted farm equipment.

DASH

The only contemporary part of the Summer House and Studio complex, the low-slung library serves as a connector between the original 1740 barn and the residential section. For many years, the railing at the top was painted white, not yellow.

ABOVE
In the late summer, plantings in the Secret Garden practically press against the low picture window in the red living room.

OPPOSITE
Dash used vintage barn doors to separate the rooms in the private quarters.

Seen from the Potager and framed by a trellised walkway, the bedroom wing comprises two attached nineteenth-century sheds.

Madoo, August 1973

by Douglas Crase

Although Madoo is famous for making an indelible first impression, my own first impression was perhaps atypical—not because we arrived under cover of darkness, but because I'd never heard of the Hamptons. It was August 1973; I was recently sprung from the Midwest and traveling for the weekend with [poet] John Ashbery, who suggested simply that we visit a painter friend "out on Long Island."

By that formula, Madoo might have been anyplace. Of course, one could see at the door that it wasn't anyplace inside. John hadn't prepared me for such an idiosyncratic dwelling, designed, as they say of Monticello, to fit the mind of a single genius. The designer in this case was the painter friend himself, Robert Dash, introduced immediately as Bob. From the grand vault of his studio, now the gallery, Bob led us to an equally lofty but narrow parlor and on to the book-lined hallway and living quarters beyond. The books, the plants, the one-of-a-kind furnishings—not to mention the art and poems displayed on the walls—all seized my attention. Nothing was fake, standard, or ordinary. But for all I knew, with the surroundings hidden in the dark, we might have been in any of the suburbs we passed by during our long ride from the city.

Even in the morning the dislocation lingered, in part because the garden continued so seamlessly from the house. If there was a neighborhood out there, I couldn't see it. We were isolated by hedges from the road to the east and bordered by potato fields that stretched toward the ocean on the south and pond on the west. According to Bob, who provided a history lesson with breakfast, we were at the center of a farming community where the loam was the most fertile in the whole country. His neighbors had worked the adjoining fields for generations. I fell hard for his stories, picturing myself in a thrifty village whose seventeenth-century roots sustained it still.

I'm not sure when the illusion fell away, but it could not have survived the party Bob hosted that Sunday, a joint birthday celebration for Ashbery and the painter Darragh Park. The studio filled with glamorous people, the cigarette smoke grew dense, the noise level ascended higher than the beams overhead. Every face was a discovery to be matched to one of the exalted names already familiar from New York School poet-and-painter lore. Suddenly, I found myself face to face with James Schuyler, a poet who in my pantheon had no peer. His companion that evening was Ruth Kligman, the girlfriend once of Pollock and later of de Kooning; she had brought Schuyler to the party from Fairfield Porter's house, where he frequently stayed while the Porters were away in Maine. The poet Kenneth Koch was in the crowd, as were the luminous Ellen Adler and Cornelia Foss. To judge by the buzz in the room, de Kooning himself may have been present.

In this circa 1975 photograph, Robert Dash and Douglas Crase walk down the driveway at Madoo. [Credit: Frank Polach]

Bob didn't read of these people in a book as I had done. He once worked in person with de Kooning, shared a studio with Porter, traveled with Alex Katz to Maine. He was a student in New Mexico when he met fellow student and painter Connie Fox. Soon he would be a friend and ally of Robert Storr, a young painter-critic whose career at the Museum of Modern Art and later as dean at the Yale School of Art then lay ahead. When Bob regaled us with his good-natured but wicked gossip, the great reputations were personalized as Bill and Fairfield, Connie and Rob and Alex. To a novitiate, the close-ups were thrilling. Even the divisions were thrilling, such that former friends and rivals—Jane Freilicher and Larry Rivers chief among them—still figured in the aesthetic coordinates one could absorb just by watching and listening at Madoo.

When the glamorous guests were gone, the enduring glamour of their art and poetry remained. On a table in the long hallway was an Alex Katz cutout of Bob in his youth (modest, but on first sight it took your breath away—shouldn't it be in a museum?), while placed like an icon among the books was a Katz collage I assumed was a portrait of Bob's impetuous Airedale, Klaxxon. There was an emblematic, gift-sized drawing from de Kooning not far from works by friends Polly Kraft and, later, Priscilla Bowden. Propped on a cabinet in the guest bathroom was an allusive Porter landscape, recognizable, once I knew more about where we were, as the Porters' house in Southampton. I confess to thinking how neatly it might fit in a suitcase. Perhaps my favorite was an unforgettable Joe Brainard piece that hung, memorably enough, next to the toilet.

OPPOSITE
In 1972, Dash and the future Pulitzer Prize–winning poet James Schuyler collaborated on a suite of six lithographs combining imagery of Madoo by Dash and lines from Schuyler's diaries. [Credit: Gary J. Mamay]

The place would have been a conservator's nightmare. It was also a young poet's paradise. The intimate presentations took the piety out of art, an effect of genius that made art seem as instinctive as breathing and as necessary.

In Bob's own work the lineage from Porter was evident, but attenuated, which led some viewers to conclude that his paintings represented a retreat from the psychological gravity his older mentor could achieve. The comparison misses the point of what must have been a hard-won independence. Where Porter's work was humanist, even anthropomorphic, Bob's became austere, a product of his appreciation for nature's complete indifference to the human presence. This wasn't cynicism on his part, or nihilism, but an active sympathy for the otherness of nature, a celebration of its psychological emptiness. Perhaps he derived this insight from gardening, perhaps from his time in New Mexico. The year before my first visit, he printed a set of six lithographs that made his position explicit. Each lithograph was keyed to a line taken from Schuyler's diary and reproduced like a motto below the image. All the images were of the garden. One featured the words "Sunny and clear, pale and empty as a photograph..." It hung for a while above the kitchen sink, a daily reminder of how to perceive and, as seemed obvious even then, how to paint.

In his dual respect for visual and verbal art, Bob was true to the collegial genius of the New York School, no doubt the most useful example of that genius I would ever know. He was probably not the first in history to hang poems on the wall like paintings, but Madoo was the first place I saw it done. My introduction to the poetry of John Koethe occurred when I found a poem of his framed on Bob's Summer House wall. Other poet friends whose work appeared there included Schuyler, Ashbery, Barbara Guest, and the young Peter Schjeldahl. The confiding presence of their poems was as defining as the paintings and the garden. Bob's life—I want to say his art-felt life—simply changed the way the world looked. Or, to be more accurate, it changed the way one saw the world, just as we know real poetry not for what it says but because it changes the way we hear. I would take that lesson from Madoo wherever I went, though it could feel at times no substitute for actually being there. In his poem "Alive in the Hamptons," Gerrit Henry explored his own feelings about Bob's great creation. His conclusion, which must speak for many of us, was expressed in a single unambiguous line: "I still find it wonderful, still sigh to live this way."

Douglas Crase, a poet and essayist based in New York City, is a former MacArthur Fellow and a Whiting Award recipient.

Sunny and clear, pale and empty as a photograph…

CHAPTER FOUR

The Pompeiian Court

A pair of griffins stand sentry on the Pompeiian Court. Yellow lilies, pink malvas, and variegated Solomon's seal grow within the boxwood enclosure. The area is set off by three screens painted watermelon and chocolaty purple.

At the far side of the pond, the woodland garden and the Pompeiian Court sneak up on a visitor. That they appear almost by osmosis might be among the most important aspects of Dash's design credo. In grand English garden parlance, they would be called "rooms," but in truth they are more indistinct spaces. These and other small structures or special planting areas, typically no more than 10 feet square, form discrete compositions peppered throughout Madoo, each slipping its way into another, the sum total of which is key to the magic that makes the garden appear much larger than its 2 acres.

Books in Dash's personal library often reference the ancient world, but the reason he created the Pompeiian Court is not known, although he did travel to Italy in the 1960s with friends including the writer and Italophile Gore Vidal. Designed with a purpose in mind, the Pompeiian Court serves an interstitial task, tethering the old Loo shed to the Ginkgo Grove in one direction and to the Summer House in another, neatly bisected by telephone pole paths. Paved with large river rocks, this quadrant mimics ancient stone-slab roadbeds and is difficult to navigate. The "foot feel" here is very different from any other part of Madoo, and you have to pay attention as you walk, particularly when the rocks are slicked with rain. Two wooden trellis screens define the space, painted in myriad colors over the years and currently dull pink framed in purple. Dash created these screens to suggest Ornamental, a style of painting found at archaeological sites such as Pompeii and Herculaneum.

The planted area comprises a simple rectangle of narrow boxwood hedging fronted by four brown Korean ceramic pots that mimic ancient oil jars. They are often planted with caladiums and occasionally house dramatic bromeliads with almost iridescent pink centers that evoke the potted agaves seen in so many Italian gardens. Faux stone griffins flank the sides, one of them edged with a slow-growing, yellow-leaved Boston ivy (*Parthenocissus tricuspidata*) that delicately obscures the sculpture by autumn. A reproduction Roman faun statue once occupied the rectangle's center, although it disappeared long ago. In its place, we positioned a cast-stone obelisk, which has moved hither and yon over the decades at Madoo, including a stint punctuating the Rill in the 1980s. A spreading clump of variegated Solomon's seal (*Polygonatum odoratum*) and a lovely pale silvery pink malva grow within the confines of the rectangular hedging.

Aside from a giant fastigiate oak, the tree selection in and around the Pompeiian Court has little to do with the ancient world. Pawpaw trees (*Asimina triloba*) with burgundy-brown blossoms in the spring and yellow-green fruit in the late autumn are favored by the squirrels and occasionally by humans for making custards and pies. (Native to North America, the pawpaw is also known as "northern banana.") A single-stem *Cryptomeria*, its trunk wrapped in a variegated

MADOO SAGGAPONNACK N Y 11962

I am trying a Pompeiian room at Madoo: pots, screens, river-washed stones, two winged gryphons, and a bronze satyr from Naples. Mountain laurel will do for myrtle, but I desperately need a toga.

--R. D.

OPPOSITE
A view of Madoo's brand-new Welcome Center, on the site of the former Loo shed. The mirrors reflect the garden and repositioned stone pavers now interplanted with *Juncus greenei*, *Lobelia siphilitica*, and *Dianthus petraeus*. A pair of potted citrus trees amplify the Greco-Roman vibe.

CLOCKWISE FROM NEAR RIGHT
A pair of painted iron pineapple finials mounted on wooden posts mark the entrance to a path that wends its way toward the Pompeiian Court. Masses of bishop's-weed brighten an area beneath a Spanish fir.

The main telephone pole path splits in two, with one branch leading toward the Asian Pond Garden. At right, a *Stewartia pseudocamellia* rises from a planting of *Stephanandra incisa*.

The obelisk once punctuated the Rill and was later relocated to the Pompeiian Court.

Euonymus, towers above hundreds of *Petasites japonicus*, which produce showy bulbous flower cones in the spring that later unfurl into a sea of large paddle-shaped leaves. Alongside a portion of the telephone pole path, several dying thujas were removed a few years ago to make way for a new collection of fall- and spring-blooming camellias, which have taken well to this protected shady area, despite occasional incursions by pesky deer. Ultimately, they'll provide a sense of enclosure that Dash had previously attempted with the lush thujas, creating an almost tropical forest effect.

These are underplanted with ferns, hellebores, and a variegated *Carex* that brings some light color to the dark shadows. Here, the change from fall-blooming to winter-blooming plants is most noticeable. The autumn-blooming camellias close out the primary floral season just as the early-blooming *Helleborus niger*, or Christmas rose, reveals its parchment-like petals maybe a month before the much-anticipated snowdrops poke their heads up and make themselves known in early winter.

Beneath the *Cryptomeria*'s arching limbs lies a short path to the Temple or, as Dash used to call it, the *templum barbecueum*. A simple structure originally intended to resemble the Temple of Vesta, it is fully functional for summer grilling, although it is most often used to roast

MADOO SAGGAPONNACK N Y 11962

And underneath heavy shrubberies one might have shoals and fingering peninsulas of bulbs late in the season, for here ice will stay and stay and extend the bloom of the earliest snowdrops well into tulip time. With ample spring winds, sunlight will filter down through shrub-sway enough for them to mature and form buds in their bulbs for the following year, although this is always a bit of a risk.

--R. D.

OPPOSITE, CLOCKWISE FROM NEAR RIGHT
Wisteria blooms atop the Temple in sync with Spanish bluebells (*Hyacinthoides hispanica*) at ground level.

A simple black wrought-iron gate leads to the Temple. Wispy 'September Charm' anemones and pawpaw trees, an American native, add to the atmospherics.

Adjacent to the Temple and embracing one of the upright beeches in the Beech Glade is *Corylopsis pauciflora*, which has pale chartreuse blossoms and was favored by Dash over bright yellow forsythia, which he disdained.

chestnuts in winter. The octagonal structure has changed in recent years: Curved concrete tables that once surrounded the formerly brick firepit have been removed, and its short, narrow walls have been topped by slightly wider, more comfortable cedar seats surrounding a Cor-Ten steel firebowl made by Elena Colombo, a local artisan. The concrete columns were formed by Sonotubes, their brutalist rusticity somewhat softened by a swirling hive of wisteria vines that encircles the Temple's top. In the late spring, they erupt in a cloud of lavender, eventually showering the ground with pastel petals cast off by their racemes.

A jumble of shrubs planted at one side of the Temple's entrance suggests age. A *Hamamelis virginiana* leans into a *Taxus* that has grown quite tall: Dash planned for them to abut each other so that the minuscule yellow blossoms of the witch hazel would pop more brightly against the *Taxus*'s evergreen needles. But he didn't plan for their long-term growth and, as a result, both plants require annual pruning to retain their intentional shapes.

Large clumps of *Galanthus nivalis*, a snowdrop with gray-green leaves, dot the berm to the left of the path to the office alongside a sculpturally pruned lacebark pine (*Pinus bungeana*), so named for its camouflage-like skin, which shimmers on wet winter days. The snowdrops lie directly beneath the *Stephanandra incisa*, just as prescribed by Dash, who deemed the see-through wiry structure of the shrubs an ideal protective sheath for the small ephemeral spring bulbs. The snowdrops now grow by the thousands, descendants of just a handful of bulbs planted one fall many years ago, and hidden clumps have been divided and replanted "in the green," after they've

CLOCKWISE FROM ABOVE
In this circa 1996 picture, a topiary form encages a small sculpture of a satyr in the center of the boxwood rectangle, flanked by the griffins. The former Loo shed lies beyond. [Credit: Wendy Goodrich]

Camellia × 'Snow Flurry', which blooms from mid-October through early winter, and potted *Euphorbia* 'Diamond Frost' face the Pompeiian Court.

A grove of camellias flanks the path to the Temple. *Camellia japonica* 'April Dawn' has blooms described as candy-caned in white and pink, but colors from white to coral-red can appear on the same plant and vary from year to year. A pair of Seibert & Rice pots, inscribed with poetry by Dash, and a *Hamamelis virginiana*, its trunk purposefully trained akimbo to suggest age, complete the tableau. [Credit: Alejandro Saralegui]

OPPOSITE
A delicate tracery of blooming *Akebia quinata* cascades from the former Loo shed's roof.

flowered but still retain their leaves, the best way to encourage future productivity. Scattered along the berm adjacent to the Ginkgo Grove and given a light dose of tomato fertilizer, they bloom beautifully every winter, a carpet of snow among the limbed-up rhododendrons and a dramatic counterpoint to the willowy ginkgo trunks.

Most of the snowdrops were planted before galanthomania took hold among bulb enthusiasts, so it's difficult to identify all the cultivars. Some bear an unexpectedly large leaf or petal, distinct markings, or a pale green blush on the outer foliage. A local galanthophile identified one with good poise and a slightly corrugated leaf: We might just decide to call it *Galanthus nivalis* 'Madoo'.

The Pompeiian Court is reached via Dash's signature telephone pole paths, a seemingly inexpensive paving option that over time proved anything but. Dash lamented that the original wood, before being cut into paving disks, was so hard it quickly ruined sawblades. Today, it is difficult to acquire old telephone poles for replacement material, as utility companies are hesitant to distribute them to consumers because they are soaked in creosote. But when Madoo's garden crew cheats and uses discarded tree trunks instead, the disks disintegrate quickly. So, telephone poles it is.

A telephone pole walkway mimics the shape of paths that Dash mowed when Madoo was mostly meadow. Narrow *Taxus* hedges and liriope flank the edges.

ABOVE
A sea of *Petasites japonicus*, hemmed in by the telephone pole path, floats on a berm planted with limbed-up rhododendrons.

OPPOSITE, LEFT TO RIGHT
Euonymus petals litter the telephone pole path near the entrance to the Temple. The camellias on the right are underplanted with clumps of *Carex siderosticta* 'Variegata'.

The limbed rhododendron trunks stretch skyward above the large paddle-like *Petasites japonicus*.

A foggy morning blends the springtime colors of the lacebark pine (*Pinus bungeana*), *Petasites japonicus*, and *Corylopsis pauciflora*. The path here features a pattern of zigzag brick and telephone pole disks.

CHAPTER FIVE

The Ginkgo Grove and the Beech Glade

The fan-shaped leaves of the ginkgoes filter the sunlight on an early fall afternoon. The trees were planted as 6-foot-tall saplings in the early 1980s and are anchored by a mature set of boxwood balls.

Madoo's most modern aspect might likely be the Ginkgo Grove: a brace of fastigiate ginkgoes that grow seemingly haphazardly and without purpose, a smattering of boxwood balls nipping at their bases. Originally planted in grass, as saplings the ginkgoes were barely noticeable, their thunder stolen by the showy lavender Gazebo nearby. But at some point, Dash removed the grass to make mulched paths and had the trees pruned severely to form narrow spires reaching like church steeples toward the sky. The trees lie both within and outside the paths' borders, creating a slightly disorienting funhouse effect. Walking among them is, as many visitors have noticed over the years, similar to the feeling Alice must have had when she tumbled down the rabbit hole.

A few years after Dash's death, the dark mulch was replaced with lighter-hued ground stone, making the composition brighter and giving it a crisper edge. The once frivolous, come-what-may experiment has evolved into the principal feature of Madoo, serving as a crucial transition point between the garden's front and back acres. It's worth noting that no matter which path one takes at Madoo, you have to go through the Ginkgo Grove at least twice to take everything in. If a figure eight were to be laid on the property, the grove would occupy the very center, wholly intentional if not immediately apparent.

Dash was interested in ancient trees, and ginkgoes are among the oldest on earth. (Some fossilized specimens date from 170 million years ago.) Intriguingly, they were thought to be extinct in the wild until the early twentieth century, and by the 1970s their leaves had been immortalized by jeweler Angela Cummings in pieces that she designed for Tiffany & Co. Ginkgoes are essentially conifers with deciduous leaves that harbor vestigial needles—they simply happened to stop evolving much further about 35 to 55 million years ago. Today, they are more familiarly known for their fruit, considered an aphrodisiac and memory aid, the efficacy of which is continually disputed.

Madoo's ginkgoes have matured beautifully. Every other spring, the gardeners don climbing gear, shimmy up the trees' narrow flanks, and prune them so that they spread no wider than 4 to 5 feet across from branch to branch, including their trunks. Witnessing the process involves a bit of hand-wringing, as the gardeners start on the strongest tree and then stretch across to the others with a telescoping pruning saw until all eleven are done. A few years ago, we decided to top them, as they would be impossible to prune if they were to grow any taller.

The berm that was created when the Winter Studio and Conservancy office were built flanks one side of the grove, its abrupt slope studded with rhododendrons. An unknown illness almost claimed them at one point, but the shrubs rebounded and Dash limbed them up, turning their twisted trunks into an asset. Yearly applications of peat moss (now no longer used, as it releases carbon upon being unearthed) and organic fertilizer have since kept them in good health, and today

MADOO SAGGAPONNACK N Y 11962

After an early breakfast, I had this idea of adding box balls to the composition. Rather a wild stroke. But an inspired one, perhaps a riff on Alice and her game of croquet, wherein hedgehogs are balls, bent playing cards (courtiers) hoops.

--R. D.

their sinuous forms have coalesced into an attractive mixed-shade ground cover. Newer limbed-up rhododendrons have been added over time, with a trunk or two removed each year; eventually, they will blend in and outpace the originals. As the *Petasites japonicus* peter out from the telephone pole path, the ground cover changes to a mix of bulbs and perennials that shine in the spring, along with a sensitive fern (*Onoclea sensibilis*), transplanted here from elsewhere in the garden and now sprouting up by itself.

The Beech Glade stands in the somewhat undefined area between the Ginkgo Grove and the Summer House, anchored by a pair of mismatched fastigiate 'Dawyck Gold' beeches. The renovation of this swath of Madoo began with a "river" of variegated *Acorus* (*A. gramineus* 'Variegatus'). There had been a 5-foot-square patch of the *Acorus* with a sad pink rose at its center, but it seemed superfluous. So, one spring we weeded the glade, removing a failing curly willow in the process. Suddenly, the giant upright beeches made themselves known, along with a roughly delineated axis between the Gazebo and a *Magnolia grandiflora* planted at the southwest corner of the Summer House. Opened up to the sun and the sky, the patch transformed into a true river: The gardeners divided the small square of *Acorus* into clumps and planted them within a flagged section that now reveals a new perspective of Madoo from all angles, while doubling as a subtle connective device.

A pair of trees nearby have so little in common that one has to wonder what Dash was thinking when he planted them. One, a multistemmed magnolia, has grown to shade an entire end of the Beech Glade and the *Acer griseum* planted adjacent to it. Both are wonderful trees, with strikingly contrasting bark color and texture: the magnolia all mottled grays and smooth to the touch, and the *Acer* notable for its cinnamon-hued, unfurling papery bark. This juxtaposition is an educational moment, especially in the winter, when the windswept Long Island landscape calls attention to hidden beauties that would otherwise never be picked to dance.

CLOCKWISE FROM ABOVE

A snowfall makes this modernist composition even more minimalist by obscuring the pathways and lawn.

A skyward view of the ginkgoes' spires in winter. Every other spring, the trees' branches are pruned to about 12 inches in length.

The grove offers a safe harbor for a pair of squirrel's nests.

Ginkgo leaves carpet the pathway and the tops of the boxwood balls in late fall.

OPPOSITE
Paths through the Ginkgo Grove were created long after the trees were planted. A clump of gooseneck loosestrife next to the Gazebo is routinely managed to keep it from spreading.

BELOW
The ginkgoes in autumn, just as they start to drop their leaves. The grove is flanked by a variegated arborvitae and an *Acer griseum*.

RIGHT
With the berm as a backdrop, a group of trees in early spring reveal their structure. Far left to right: the Ginkgo Grove, an *Acer griseum*, a large multi-stemmed magnolia, and an aged crab apple tree.

BELOW RIGHT
The lopsided growth of the ginkgo at left can be attributed to the *Magnolia × soulangeana* at the right, which has outpaced the slender tree.

CLOCKWISE FROM TOP
In spring 2024, the berm had only a few awkwardly placed clumps of snowdrops. We decided to experiment by dividing several clumps of snowdrops (early in the season, rather than after blooming) and planting them in smaller groups to fill out the space more evenly.

The berm in midspring, with a ground cover of hellebores, daffodils, summer snowflakes, violets, heuchera, and ferns. As we find leggy rhododendrons, we'll add them here, since the originals are beginning to die out.

A group of snowdrops in the berm, ready for dividing

OPPOSITE
An Ice N' Roses 'Early Red' hellebore grows on the berm near the ginkgoes.

MADOO SAGGAPONNACK N Y 11962

Freckled shadows are both merry and grave. The tissue-paper *rugosa* rose 'Blanc Double de Coubert' is not cream, not skimmed milk, but rain-free cumulus-cloud white, always suggesting a clear, clear day. It is so notably free of fugitive tint that it will darken surrounding foliage and not the other way round, or make surrounding leaves seem fresher. And though its own foliage has undiminished, ingratiating freshness, going from apple green when young to almost mature apple when older and then, in autumn, to the most brilliant high ocher, the flowers are always the superior color of the finest white bond.

--R. D.

OPPOSITE
At the edge of the Beech Glade lies a swath of *Rosa rugosa* 'Blanc Double de Coubert', a Dash favorite, punctuated by a rustic, stone-studded concrete birdbath.

RIGHT
The Beech Glade features two fastigiate 'Dawyck Gold' beeches that share the same name but are quite different in habit. In front, a *Magnolia stellata* echoes the beeches' burnished autumnal tones.

BELOW
Spring unfurls in the Beech Glade as the early-blooming *Magnolia stellata* fades and the *M.* × *soulangeana* begins its bright pink show.

LEFT
Tassels of lemon-yellow *Corylopsis spicata* also brighten the Beech Glade during early spring.

ABOVE
The astilbes in all their summer glory. After the flowers have faded, the plants are not deadheaded, as the seed heads are attractive through the winter.

OPPOSITE
Teasels stretch toward the sun above cinnamon-and-yellow daylilies at the edge of the Beech Glade.

A "river" of *Acorus gramineus* 'Variegatus' was planted within the Beech Glade to connect the Summer House and the Gazebo while highlighting the glade's namesake trees. *Astilbe chinensis* 'Vision in Red' grows to one side of the *Acorus*; the Summer House lies beyond.

CHAPTER SIX

The Quincunx Gardens and the Hornbeam Bower

The quincunx *Taxus* have been stripped of their leaves by deer to about 5 feet. During rutting season, the trunks are protected with twine. In the second bed, a seven-son flower (*Heptacodium miconioides*) remains from a previous planting, now too large to move.

The almost claustrophobic, tightly stitched together Ginkgo Grove gives way to the much airier back half of the property, also known as the Winter House lawn, which is mapped out more strictly than most of the rest of Madoo. During the colder months, Dash lived in the Winter House—the 1850 barn that had once been attached to the northern end of what is now the Summer Studio—and his view from the dining room windows was largely architectural in scope and mostly leafless.

Running alongside the Long Border on the lawn's eastern side, the Quincunx Gardens are decidedly controlled, with a limited plant palette. Started as four short, square boxwood shrubberies with a quincunx pattern—a medieval planting design for orchards—they featured a *Taxus* in each corner and one in the center, not unlike five pips on a die. (The word "quincunx" derives from an ancient Roman-era coin that bore five dots in the same pattern and weighed five-twelfths of a libra.) In orchards, as at Madoo, the form ensures regularity and formality: The *Taxus* read as straight lines any which way you look at them.

When they were first planted, each bed featured a mix of textures courtesy of golden cypresses (*Chamaecyparis pisifera* 'Aurea'), a *Poncirus trifoliata*, and a few oddities like a *Heptacodium miconioides* (seven-son flower), some asparagus, and a black pussy willow. Over the years, Dash added more shrubs within the boxwood squares, and the plants began to shade each other out. By the time it was decided to renovate this area, the proper quincunx structure was all but lost. The golden cypresses had grown into 8-foot-tall trees practically bare from the top down, and the seven-son flower was almost 20 feet tall. The beds had become an ungainly mass of spindly, sun-starved branches, and even the stalwart *Taxus* had gone through degradations as deer stripped their trunks bare. But rather than finding fault, Dash decided to make a feature of the latter's chipped red-and-gray trunks, putting a mischievous spin on the quotidian *Taxus* found in traditional suburban foundation plantings.

The effort to replant the quincunx beds called for retaining the original concept of the five *Taxus* in each square. In came the gardeners and out went the truly dead matter, discarded into the compost pile. The golden cypresses were limbed up in hopes of turning them into topiary standards for a future project, and any salvageable plants were relocated to the Long Border. The *Poncirus*, notable for their sinister sharp thorns, were traded for other plant material from a local nursery (only one was retained, also making its new home in the Long Border).

The now bare gardens—aside from the *Taxus* and the seven-son flower, which was too large to move—were ready to be replanted. *Calamagrostis brachytricha* is a grass that can stand practically at attention year-round, and its late-summer blooms are tall enough to clear the boxwood hedges. We also added *Echinacea pallida* for a bit of midsummer color and *Kalimeris pinnatifida* 'Hortensis', with its white pincushion-like double flower, for a shrubbier contrast. Within a year, the

MADOO SAGGAPONNACK N Y 11962

It is to the Greek traveler and philosopher Xenophon that we owe the quincunx plan. He claims to have seen it in the gardens of Cyrus the Great, the illustrious Persian, although Xenophon did have an annoying habit of writing about places he had never visited. What it is is a device for creating light and shadow in the desert. Trees are placed toward the corners of a perfect square and one is installed dead center. They then are limbed up and cubed, the resulting masses creating an enfilade of light and shadow. It was a place where people sat or strolled and were refreshed.

--R. D.

RIGHT
In front of the Hornbeam Bower, granite faux bois stumps from a cemetery plot in upstate New York are positioned haphazardly, some straight up and others sinking into the ground at odd angles. A symbol of eternity and humanity, the faux bois motif was popularized in cemeteries in the late nineteenth century.

OPPOSITE
The *Taxus*, cubed to give them a more formal presence, have merged, forming archways and creating a highly detailed framework above multilayered plantings below.

Calamagrostis brachytricha had begun to overshadow the latter plantings. After the grasses are cut down in March, there's just enough time for the *Narcissus poeticus* to bloom, with ivory *Camassia* following just a few weeks later. The new scheme is simpler and easier to maintain, but just as striking and effective as the original. Accordingly, the *Taxus* have been sheared from their more natural flame shape to rectangular cubes atop their deer-manipulated trunks. Viewed from a distance, they read like soldiers, Andre Le Nôtre style.

Due north of the four quincunx beds, the Hornbeam Bower routinely draws oohs and aahs from visitors and serves as the site of many a wedding. Like most other trees at Madoo, the six little-leaf hornbeams were planted as saplings, barely 6 feet tall. Hornbeams take to shearing well and have been used for centuries in northern European gardens to create architectural interest in landscapes, from tunnels to walls to coves. Dash wired Madoo's together to form an arched arbor, which finally coalesced about a decade after being planted. The trees' leaders are no longer visible, and twice-yearly shearing maintains the shape of the invitingly curved bower's merged branches.

Directly in front of the Hornbeam Bower, six randomly placed faux bois tree stumps poke out of the ground. Carved from granite and heavy as hell (most faux bois garden ornamentation is made from molded cement), they once graced a nineteenth-century cemetery plot in upstate New York and were gifted to Madoo by a neighbor. Upon their delivery, the gardeners asked Dash where he'd like them positioned. From his seat at the Winter House dining table, Dash exclaimed, "Do it yourself. Just pretend you're drunk!" And so, one trunk is upright, another half-buried, and yet another at a 40-degree angle, with the remaining three juxtapositioned just as differently. Today, more than thirty years later, the gardeners still call them *los borrachos*—the drunkards—and children gleefully climb on and jump off them, a source of simple joy. Ancient Rome, medieval Europe, classical garden parks, American cemeteries: In just a 40-yard-long stretch, Madoo can be a startling mash-up that somehow flows effortlessly. It's a garden with very few hard stops.

In late spring, the boxwood-edged quincunx beds bloom with the fragrant *Narcissus* 'Actaea'. Each of the four quincunx beds is defined by five *Taxus*, one in each corner and one in the center.

ABOVE
A mere 5 feet separates the formal Quincunx Gardens from the informal Long Border, but they coexist in harmony given the preponderance of greens.

OPPOSITE
A cast-stone urn under the Hornbeam Bower is planted with a bird's-nest fern that overwinters each year in the greenhouse.

OPPOSITE
Winter sunlight catches the tawny seed heads of the *Calamagrostis brachytricha*, which is left untouched until the daffodils start to sprout.

RIGHT
The structure of the Hornbeam Bower is more readily understood on winter days, when the leaves have fallen. A poplar tree on the neighbor's property looms over the back of the Winter House lawn.

BELOW
Snow amplifies the urn's delicate tracery.

ABOVE
The stile—a device traditionally used to cross a creek or traverse a fence—has inhabited many parts of Madoo. Its current resting spot at the south end of the quincunx beds allows visitors to climb the steps for a view of the Winter House lawn, a double hedge of highbush blueberry (*Vaccinium corymbosum*) and Osage orange (*Maclura pomifera*), and the neighboring farm.

MADOO SAGGAPONNACK N Y 11962

. . . while this green flood was collecting, it soon became clear to me that this perfect color field would need some framing, and so the garden's inanimates--fences, railings, bowls, posts, arbors, doors, gates, benches, and tools--began to wear high hues of the sort that would make indoor eyeballs wince but were quite suitable outside. Didn't da Vinci say that the air does the painting?

--R. D.

OPPOSITE
Previously painted black, the stile now sports a coat of dark grape and lavender, topped off with jaunty finials painted bright pea green.

ABOVE
Spikes of *Camassia leichtlinii* 'Semiplena' bloom within the quincunx beds while a reed grass, *Calamagrostis brachytricha*, begins to emerge from beneath.

RIGHT
The corridor between the Long Border (left) and the quincunx beds assumes a formal air, akin to a French allée. The pathway terminates at the blueberry and Osage orange double hedge.

CHAPTER SEVEN

The Long Border

OPPOSITE
Tulips planted along the length of the Long Border are chosen for both their color and bloom time, complementing the foliage of the surrounding trees and shrubs.

RIGHT
A giant pussy willow (*Salix chaenomeloides*) in late winter bloom. The tree is pollarded after it blooms, as it provides a rare food source for a variety of pollinators at this time of year.

The classic long border, a ubiquitous feature in British gardens, calls to mind Jane Austen's period characters, strolling self-admiringly on stretches of grass while taking in the verdant spread before them, or perhaps a garden party scene from *Downton Abbey*, with a seemingly endless flower border as a backdrop. The component parts of these blowsy settings are anything but frivolous, however. An evergreen wall is essential, with an invisible path in front of it so that gardeners can access the back of the border, and then perennials and shrubs, from short in the front to tall in the rear, all densely planted in repetition, repetition, repetition along the border's growth.

Notable examples include the double red borders at Hidcote Manor in Gloucestershire, created by Major Lawrence Johnston in the early twentieth century, which culminate in a pair of redbrick peak-roofed pavilions. One of the sultrier garden sights in England, it was reputedly inspired by *Madame Suggia*, a painting by Augustus John: The carmine flowers and dark foliage of the 'Bishop of Llandaff' dahlias, the burgundy-leaved *Cordyline australis*, and purple sage all reflect the bright to dark reds found in Madame's gown. More traditional is Gertrude Jekyll's flower border at Munstead Wood in Sussex, which runs longer than 200 feet with a stone wall, not an evergreen one, at the back. And at Great Dixter, also in Sussex, the long border first created by Christopher Lloyd and now overseen by Fergus Garrett is a constant experiment, fittingly long and filled with mostly herbaceous plants but also featuring bold jolts of color and visual interest year-round—although it originally had a more truncated bloom period from April to October. Early on, Great Dixter's border broke with tradition. Lloyd wrote: "The effect should be of a closely woven tapestry. I do not at all mind bringing some tall plants to the border's front, so long as an open texture allows the eye to see past them. Conversely, channels of low growth can be allowed, at times, to run to the back of the border."

Madoo's Long Border is altogether different. It originated in the early 1980s as a minimalist planting of *Rosa* 'Fru Dagmar Hastrup' adjacent to one length of the Winter House lawn, a simple solution to delineate

CLOCKWISE FROM NEAR RIGHT
Brilliant purple beautyberries (*Callicarpa americana*) shine against the mottled gray bark of a magnolia tree.

The Japanese maple is carefully pruned to retain its shape and footprint, its color enhanced by the mahogany and burgundy leaves of the oakleaf hydrangea below.

Late autumn sun illuminates a curly willow (*Salix matsudana* 'Tortuosa') and a Swedish-blue wheel-away bench on the Winter House lawn.

OPPOSITE
The bark of the handkerchief tree and the Japanese maple contrast just as much as the leaves do.

the north-south property line opposite the neighboring farm field. Dash then added poplars—inexpensive and short-lived, but fast-growing—to add drama and definition, along with a bit of a nod to Monet's famous paintings of poplars lining the banks of the Epte River. Dash gave these a boost with 20-inch-tall fastigiate golden beech tree saplings (*Fagus sylvatica* 'Dawyck Gold'), which have since matured to 20 feet and higher. A few of the smaller ones were later moved to the Winter House lawn's western border alongside the stilted linden hedge. The last of the poplars came down in 2018.

More diverse trees were subsequently integrated here and there: a golden honey locust (*Gleditsia triacanthos*), which now towers over the entire area and competes with the massive tulip tree (*Liriodendron*) that looms above the border's northeastern corner, three magnolias, a red-leaved Japanese maple (*Acer palmatum*), a handkerchief tree (*Davidia involucrata*), an upright English oak (*Quercus robur* f. *fastigiata*), and a Chinese fringe tree (*Chionanthus retusus*). As of this writing, the original roses have all but disappeared, most likely shaded out by younger trees and shrubs.

The plantings are a compelling mix, to be sure—a collector's selection, even—but hardly the makings of a cohesive long border.

ABOVE
The handkerchief tree's unique inflorescences are composed of two large ivory-colored bracts protecting a cluster of flowers inside. The bracts act as petals, attracting pollinators. In the autumn, the tree produces a hard, almost round nut containing seeds.

OPPOSITE
The branches of the handkerchief tree, studded with blossoms. *Davidia involucrata* is named for Père Armand David, a French missionary who encountered the tree in China in 1869.

And breaking with convention, the 175-foot-long boxwood hedge that defines the length of it thwarts easy access to and even an appreciation of the shorter plantings in the foreground—a design scheme which is essentially antithetical to the British model. The hedge, topped with a series of topiaried Regency swags, isn't cut with Versailles-like precision, but rather by eye, which brings it down a notch in terms of formality.

Selective editing of the trees, mostly for health reasons, has opened up a bit more sky, and varieties that once fought for attention have been pruned to live together more harmoniously, a good example being the Japanese maple and the handkerchief tree, which had been pushing against each other. The maple had begun to take over, so it was cut back drastically, giving the handkerchief tree more space to grow. The pruning is virtually imperceptible now.

When Dash gave tours of Madoo, he would pause to tell his visitors a story upon their arrival at the *Davidia*. "This is a *Davidia involucrata*," he would say authoritatively, "discovered in 1869 by Père David [Father Armand David], a French missionary, and nicknamed the 'handkerchief tree.' Had it been discovered in our time, I think we'd be calling it a Kleenex tree."

The Long Border's lower layers were addressed once the disparate assemblage of trees finally came to order. A random trunk of the doublefile viburnum was removed, and suddenly it bore the most perfect shape: Sometimes scrutiny and one fine cut are all that's needed. Much of the more delicate, considered pruning at Madoo has been left to one of our volunteers, Billy Squier, a rock musician who taught himself arborist skills in order to take care of his own Bridgehampton property and a small patch of Central Park near his New York City apartment. Once a year, Squier works his way through Madoo and gives it a little nip and a tuck.

Perennials, including previously extant Siberian iris, have divided and conquered, the iris becoming rivers of blue that connect the trees and shrubs, utterly transforming the Long Border during the week or two that they bloom. The addition of *Amsonia hubrechtii* provides a soft haze of blue flowers in the spring, then turns golden yellow in the fall and buff during the winter while enriching the border with a pleasing, feathery bulk. Likewise, *Baptisia australis* and *Veronicastrum virginicum* 'Fascination' add floral moments to the border, interesting foliage all season long, and a striking, almost black skeletal form. Various other buffs, browns, and blacks contribute to an unusual, unexpected canvas hemmed in by the bright green of the box hedge. Winter cleanup of the Long Border is now delayed until March to provide habitat for insects and food for birds and to protect the crowns of the perennials, making Madoo's border more ecologically impactful, if not quite a tapestry—or, for that matter, a bit player in a period drama.

The Long Border in late spring, as leaves emerge on trees, including a *Davidia involucrata* (handkerchief tree) and, to its right, an *Acer palmatum* (red Japanese maple). Tulips peek above the scalloped boxwood hedge, unifying the border from one end to the other.

MADOO SAGGAPONNACK N Y 11962

Peonies, I think, are the last endorsement of high spring.

--R. D.

OPPOSITE, LEFT

A single pink peony, 'Bowl of Beauty', reaches for the sun.

OPPOSITE, RIGHT

A tousled white peony starts to fade against the fuchsia blooms of *Gladiolus communis* subsp. *byzantinus*.

RIGHT

Two burgundy-colored tulips with different markings—'Doberman' (above) and 'Slawa' (below)—play against the young bronze foliage of a nearby peony.

BELOW

Jewel-toned tulips include 'Purple Dream', 'Dutch Dancer', and 'Hakuun'. Every year, about a thousand tulips are added to the Long Border in slightly different mixes. White tulips are always included to brighten the border as tree leaves begin to shade the area.

LEFT

Tulipa 'Purple Dream' was selected for its elegant lily-like shape.

OPPOSITE
The flask-shaped hips of an eglantine rose brighten the Long Border in early October. In bloom, the shrub has single pink flowers and a delightful apple-like scent when the leaves are moist.

ABOVE
The otherworldly flower heads of *Echinops sphaerocephalus* just before they bloom

BELOW
Veronicastrum virginicum 'Fascination', a native perennial, has great structure both in bloom and afterward, in addition to attractive whorled leaves. It's paired here with 'Annabelle' hydrangeas and a bright blue lacecap hydrangea, a planting scheme that is very much in the spirit of Dash.

RIGHT COLUMN, FROM TOP
The flower spikes of the *Eremurus* act as exclamation points within the garden.

Thalictrum 'Nimbus White' brightens up shadier spots throughout the Long Border.

OPPOSITE
The fruit of the hardy orange (*Poncirus trifoliata*) is remarkably bitter, but the multiseason tree has lovely white flowers in the spring and looks great after a snowfall. Just avoid the thorns.

MADOO SAGGAPONNACK N Y 11962

I have been picking the fuzzy fruits of the [*Poncirus trifoliata*] orange for putting in a pewter bowl. A strong antiseptic aroma floats from them very like Key lime and moss.

--R. D.

ABOVE
As spring progresses, the Long Border fills in with Siberian irises, a blue ribbon that connects disparate plants including peonies, mostly 'Sarah Bernhardt', and clumps of *Eremurus robustus*.

OPPOSITE, LEFT TO RIGHT
Red bee balm (*Monarda* 'Mahogany') makes a statement at the southern end of the Long Border.

'Manitoba Morning' martagon lilies and blue lacecap hydrangeas offer a fresh midsummer color combo.

An Artist's Garden

by Madison Cox

OPPOSITE
Robert Dash, *Daisies* (1969; acrylic on canvas, 60 x 60 inches). Featuring an arrangement of simple field flowers, this work was created for Dash's one-man exhibition at the Pinakothek der Moderne in Munich, Germany, in 1969. [Credit: Gary J. Mamay]

Madoo is a paragon of garden design, existing in a league of its own. Although a garden in the truest sense of the word, it challenges any genre, classification, or definition and forms an altogether original and insurgent model, rivaling in spirit the small handful of earlier twentieth-century examples that wield a considerable stronghold on garden criteria today. A garden of incredible beauty, Madoo has and will continue to have a significant and profound influence on the approach to future garden design.

Madoo is certainly an interesting place, abundantly forceful and overpowering in its diversity of impressions. A garden on a seemingly never-ending quest, it remains neither staid nor contrived, nor even restrained, but rather concerned with constant change. The overall visual impact is countered at close inspection by concealed touches of intimate delicacy and optical delight, and a multitude of sensations mirrors its founder's genuine appreciation of the arts: Painting, music, literature, and the classics all contribute to the garden's distinct and original composition.

In 1965, Robert Dash first took deed to a windblown farmstead on the rural far eastern reaches of Long Island in New York State. The flat stretch, wedged between cultivated corn and potato fields, was mainly composed of a grassy tumbling meadow with a double barn constructed of shipwrecked timber dating to 1740 and two dilapidated shacks. The ceaseless pounding of the Atlantic surf carried throughout the property, which offered occasional glimpses of the ocean. It was a challenging and tempestuous site for a garden and to a degree remains so, where only the hardiest of plant varieties are allowed into the garden schemes.

As a painter, Dash began as an Abstract Expressionist only to renounce the style later for a more pragmatic representational approach. He distinguished himself as an American Realist, with the surrounding landscapes as his subject matter. Perhaps reflecting on his early attempts to subjugate the boisterous site, Dash painted the ever-changing light and atmosphere of open fields and vegetation, although he eventually produced abstract works that reach deeper into the soul.

In his early attempts to cultivate the land, the painter enclosed the pair of shacks with an L-shaped hall providing him with a protected inner court. By the second year, the small enclosure had become a verdant jungle with a pond and colorful combinations of snapdragons, cosmos, green zinnias, purple and white petunias, and numerous varieties of daylilies. By the fifth year, Dash was hooked and ready to venture out. Detaching the smaller of the two barns, he maneuvered it across the property to the farthest side. A pair of living and work quarters were set up in each, one for the winter months and the other for summer. Tall, closely planted hedges of privet, Russian olive, and black

OPPOSITE
Robert Dash, *Untitled* (circa 1980; acrylic on linen, 50 x 50 inches). An abstracted view of the Summer House in a medley of purple and green hues. [Credit: Gary J. Mamay]

pine went in to screen out the Atlantic gales, and over the years many were limbed up, exposing their twisted dark trunks.

Madoo is about the mystery of discovery, an adventurous labyrinth for the visitor as experienced upon arrival, when even the car park offers little in the way of introducing one to the garden. Numerous possibilities become apparent as pathways and garden gates come into focus and one feels like a child again as the adventure begins. The vivid garden posts and garden benches are brightly painted chrome yellow or lime or purple, announcing the colors of a truly individual garden ideal. In this madcap place, large, river-washed white stones crunch underfoot and tall outcroppings of pink cleomes shoot up from the gravel below. Dash made a garden that initially appears comprehensible and seemingly simple, yet with each step the possibilities of direction and combination of plants, of form and color, open onto more variation and alternate routes to take, some of which require doubling back. The seeming casualness of the garden belies the juxtapositions of striking or subtle associations such as the snow-white *Clematis* 'Duchess of Edinburgh' interlaced among the frail pearly petals of a massive 'Blanc Double de Coubert' rose.

Colors from nature's palette or the artist's are routinely mixed together, as all the wooden garden features are painted in different hues throughout the seasons. A fenced vegetable patch with diagonal bands for beds and brick paths is reinforced with delphiniums and roses popping up among the cardoons, chives, and purple basil. An open grassy meadow, thick with goldenrod left uncut and tall in late summer, is planted intermittently with peonies, broom, and daylilies with scatterings of thistle and rue, creating a subtle and rich tapestry effect. A large pond that is rendered nearly invisible through the thickets of iris and bog plants is overshadowed at one end by a viewing pavilion, an ode to the mysteries of the Far East. At another end of the garden, an intense violet-painted octagonal gazebo is set near a dreamy grove of stunted ginkgo trees, their lateral branches spreading out from the topped tree crowns. A vast bed of *rugosa* roses and ornamental grasses, kept in perpetual motion from the light-filled sea breezes, sways against the dramatic skyscape beyond. And plants as diverse as berry bushes, clematis, or coral bells, once proved sturdy and strong enough for the rough-and-tumble climate, are employed as screens or hedges, accents to evergreens, or edging along a stony path.

In a world where conformity equals acceptance, Madoo cries out. It has an individualism of such an alluring brilliance that one can only stand in awe.

A garden designer based in Paris, Morocco, and New York City, Madison Cox is the president of both Fondation Pierre Bergé–Yves Saint Laurent and Fondation Jardin Majorelle. This essay is adapted from his book Artists' Gardens *(New York: Harry N. Abrams, Inc., 1993).*

CHAPTER EIGHT

The Rill and the Tapestry Rooms

After the small bulb meadow blooms, the lawn is left unmown for a few weeks to let the bulb foliage mature.

The Rill was one of the first features installed in the Winter House lawn, a large, expansive stretch that sticks out like a tongue from Madoo's original rectangular piece of land, originally planted with a hedgerow along one property line and *Rosa* 'Fru Dagmar Hastrup' along the other (a swath that evolved into the Long Border). In between them lay virtually nothing.

As with many other areas of Madoo, the Rill tells a story of transformation. Early on, it was simply a brick pathway that led toward the Foster farm at Madoo's southernmost border. Dash gradually narrowed this path, employing a classical foreshortening trick that would make it seem longer than its 120 feet as one looked toward the farm. From inside the Winter House, the Rill is roughly centered on the windows of the dining area, so that one can even consider the play on perspective beyond the confines of the garden itself.

Later, an obelisk was added at the far end, contributing further to the overall effect of the Rill being a "view swiper," as the late British gardening doyenne Rosemary Verey called it. In other words, it forced the eye to focus on the farm field and the ocean in the distance, rather than stray here and there. Dash grew accustomed to the Rill and added more pieces to it, including a brick terrace at its north end and two golden cypresses, a bright moment in the flat winter landscape. (Before committing to the trees, Dash tested out the concept by using two wooden square planters, painted a vivid purple and filled with bamboo stakes.) Rose borders soon flanked the Rill on either side, along with lilies, wispy asparagus, spring bulbs, and Queen Anne's lace. And eventually, in the early 1990s, a watercourse—the actual rill—was fitted into the middle of the brick pathway.

By this time, the priceless view was becoming usurped by newly built houses on distant potato fields, so Dash did an about-face, relocating the obelisk and punctuating the Rill with an exedra, a brick folly that mimicked ancient Greek and Roman examples of typically roofless semicircular rooms designed for conversation. The exedra at Madoo stands about 12 feet tall and features an arched roof, its ceiling tinted with dust collected from the cut brick used for the floor and walls. A sliver of mirror, positioned vertically on its interior back wall, looks like a slit offering a glimpse of the farm field beyond, but, on closer inspection, visitors realize that the mirror reflects the Rill and visually extends its reach.

Of Indo-Persian design, rills date at least as early as the fifth century, with antecedents that go back to the Phoenician era. Used as a means of irrigation, they crisscrossed fields in a foursquare pattern that was filled with diverted mountain water and released through a sluice. Ornamentally, rills are a critical component of Islamic paradise gardens and representative of the four rivers of Eden in the Old Testament. The Rill at Madoo is simpler—linear, rather than cruciform.

During his tenure, Dash added hoops across the pathway at regular intervals to suggest the arched sprays of water emanating from the rills at the Generalife in Granada, Spain. The hoops also shrank in size the

TOP
The view swiper, the predecessor to the Rill in the Winter House lawn, circa 1990. It was literally built to draw the eye out to the farm fields beyond, as though they, too, belonged to Madoo. Dash tried growing everything from roses to hops on the plumber's pipe hoops. [Credit: Robert Dash]

BOTTOM
A view of the Foster farm, with annual cosmos in bloom

MADOO SAGGAPONNACK N Y 11962

A great donnée from the High Renaissance was the forced perspective, a narrowing of a straight line to increase the sense of depth and length. A rather simple conceit used to fine effects on garden walks, no matter how modest their effect.

--R. D.

farther they were placed alongside the Rill, exaggerating its length. These were originally planted with climbing roses, which never really took. Dash also tried *Clematis tangutica* and even hops on the hoops to create vertical interest in the flat landscape. Over time, the brick pathway began to get lost in the shuffle.

An opportunity presented itself when new neighbors removed the long-established hedgerow at the westernmost edge of Madoo while building their home. Reinstating the hedgerow required significant heavy machinery, which we used to remove the decrepit Rill and its blocky plantings. All the bricks were saved and some of the best roses retained for transplantation to the Long Border. For almost two years, the Rill was completely gone, replaced by a sweep of grass lawn. Thanks to a generous grant from the Ala and Ralph Isham Family Foundation, the Rill was ultimately rebuilt with the original bricks but is now flush with the ground, lined with steel, and dotted with a series of small square pools that terminate in a round pool, all with fountains that quietly burble with recirculated water. The watercourse is edged in the salvaged brick, except the bricks are placed on their sides, creating a slightly more elevated look. In homage to the roses that once choked its length, eight brick plinths topped with round terra-cotta pots and filled with *Rosa mutabilis* are positioned along either side. Built to last, the Rill will likely outlive us all.

The hedgerow's destruction also resulted in a planting opportunity. The house being built by the new neighbors was several times larger than its predecessor and sure to loom over Madoo. First, we erected a stockade fence and planted it with English ivy, creating a green wall that has the added benefit of buffering noise and covering unsightly pool equipment. Next, a row of eighteen lindens was planted along the fence line, intended to form a flying hedge over time. To soften the severity of this planting, a series of four garden rooms was plotted out in front of the lindens, each featuring three walls of tapestry hedging: *Ilex*, hornbeam, and 'Summer Snowflake' and 'Pragense' viburnums, all planted in tight proximity and blending into one another. The rooms' openings lie directly in line with the corridors between the Quincunx Gardens,

MADOO SAGGAPONNACK N Y 11962

The exedra, a demi-lunette structure with curved roof and an oculus, flourished in fifth-century Greece as a kind of confessional. Secrets were confided within its recess, which then spirited upward through the oculus to the always mischievous gods. . . . I made only a rude sketch of the proposed addition. . . . Its color is of sawn-brick dust mixed with concrete. I thought to leave a slip of light at the back going out of the fields but instead installed a narrow mirror to pique the eye and throw a reflection of the rose walk.

--R. D.

OPPOSITE
Positioned at the southern terminus of the Rill, the exedra is a folly designed by Dash and based on ancient Greek and Roman examples of semicircular rooms employed for conversation. Most often roofless, this example features an arched roof and a ceiling tinted in brick dust from the cut brick used for the floor and walls. Seen from a distance, the mirror at the back of the exedra appears to be a slit in the wall.

creating several axes that cross the Rill and the Winter House lawn.

To the north of the linden screen, additional blocking is provided courtesy of three rather neutral-looking thujas, against which a handful of salvaged hedgerow trees shine. The glaucous needles of a Spanish fir (*Abies pinsapo*) pop distinctly against the dark green of the thujas, and the white blossoms of the *Magnolia stellata*, moved slightly to accentuate its interesting branch structure, shine brightly. One final hole in the wall was filled with three fastigiate beeches transplanted from the Long Border, bookended at the wall's southern end with a similar layout of three upright copper beeches.

At the far southwestern corner of the Winter House lawn, overlooking the farm, breezes from the ocean just a mile away and the shade of both a butternut tree and the neighbor's giant poplar offer refreshing respite on a hot summer day. In this spot, Madoo board member Charlotte Moss created a memorial for the late architect Dale Booher, a dear friend whose widow, landscape architect Lisa Stamm, contributed to the design. Fill was used to raise it 3 feet higher for a better view of the fields, and hornbeams and boxwoods cocoon it in privacy. A bench by French garden designer Louis Benech was installed for quiet contemplation, its delicate linearity giving the substantial piece a decided airiness and the entire space the suggestion of a Japanese meditation garden.

Four meticulously pruned dwarf weeping *kousa* dogwoods, planted by Dash, lie at the head of the Rill. Pots on either side of the water feature contain *Rosa mutabilis*, a species rose whose blossoms change colors from pale pink to a bright coppery orange.

OPPOSITE
A view of the southern façade of the Winter House from the exedra. The small bulb meadow was started a mere seven months before this picture was taken. Flowers include *Narcissus bulbocodium* 'Golden Bells', *N.* 'Canaliculatus', and *N.* 'Crevette.' [Credit: Timothy Heslop]

BELOW
Upon being installed in 2023, the Tapestry Rooms—seen here from the quincunx beds—were demarcated by a simple hedge of disparate shrubs. Within a year, the plantings had merged together to become thick 4-foot-tall walls.

RIGHT
A Nara bench, designed by French landscape architect Louis Benech, is positioned among hornbeam and boxwood shrubs in the southwest corner of the Winter House lawn. This tranquil space was designed as a viewing mound and as a memorial to the late architect Dale Booher.

BELOW RIGHT
A detail of the highbush blueberry that forms part of the double hedge on either side of the exedra along the Winter House lawn's southern border

NABOKOV
NABOKOV

CHAPTER NINE

The Winter House

OPPOSITE
The Winter House's hand-crafted, sculptural spiral staircase was constructed from trees and branches felled by Hurricane Gloria. It features a handrail made of a single bittersweet vine and leads to two small loft guest rooms.

RIGHT
The aptly named 'Nevada' rose—*nevada* meaning "snowy" in Spanish—was introduced by a Spaniard, Pedro Dot, in 1927. In early June, the shrub is covered in white single blossoms. [Credit: Timothy Heslop]

When Dash moved from the Summer House to the Winter House, typically in mid-October, it was all-hands-on-deck. The gardeners were summoned with barely a day's notice and the packing began. Clothing—Dash's wardrobe comprised countless pairs of Levi's, multiple denim shirts, and New Balance sneakers—was relocated to a barely noticeable closet behind a mirrored jib door, and some artwork and a few poems that caught his fancy were hung on the walls with pushpins. The kitchen was emptied and all foodstuffs moved, along with the books he was reading or planning on reading, plus his Merriam-Webster dictionary. And the recording on the Summer House answering machine was updated to a very curt, "Calls are now taken by -3787." If you didn't know the area code or the local exchange prefix, then no need to bother.

This twice-yearly transfer—from the Summer House to the Winter House in the autumn and vice versa in the spring—represented the bulk of Dash's travel during the forty-six years he lived at Madoo, his books and imagination providing more than enough diversion. So why the move? The Winter House, which parrots the farmhouse aesthetic of Dash's summer quarters, is smaller and less expensive to heat. The inside is open plan, with a bathroom tucked in the corner, a kitchen in another corner, a sleeping area, and small sitting and dining areas. A pair of tiny, awkward guest bedrooms occupy a loft on the tightly peaked second floor.

Its current state is much as Dash left it when he died in 2013. The floors are yellow and blue spatter-dash—similar to the flooring in the Summer House—although the wall color, once shiny black, is now a more agreeable white. The wooden-keyed Chickering & Sons piano still stands by the front door, and Dash's parents' wicker, most likely from their summerhouse in Tuxedo Park, has burlap-covered seat cushions and a coral-orange paint color.

In 1985, Hurricane Gloria tore through the northeastern United States, leaving a swath of destruction in its wake. Madoo survived, but trees all over Long Island's East End did not. Dash commissioned a friend, carpenter Ralph D'Amato, to build a bed frame and a spiral staircase from deadwood felled by the storm. The bed, essentially a four-poster on

MADOO SAGGAPONNACK N Y 11962

Work is to begin. The joy of it. The immutable pilgrim silence of it. The doubts. "What do you do here, in winter," said Lee Krasner. "Count pheasant feathers?" I guess. And not too many. It's always a dull moment. Those who stay know it. Those who were born here know it. Here is still here and will be, always.

--R. D.

OPPOSITE
Gifts to Dash that used to hang on the walls of the Summer and Winter houses are now displayed in the Winter Studio, where Dash painted while he was in residence. Among the works are pieces by Alex Katz, Willem de Kooning, Fairfield Porter, Robert Kulicke, Polly Kraft, Jane Freilicher, Rebecca Purdum, and Lee Krasner. Dash wrote his column for the *East Hampton Star* on the manual typewriter. [Credit: Gary J. Mamay]

steroids, has wheelbarrow wheels for legs and a framework of gnarled branches reaching up from each corner, nearly touching the ceiling. D'Amato created the spiral staircase (it replaced a utilitarian factory ladder) from a single tree trunk that also rises toward the ceiling, with triangular solid-wood treads spinning off it at irregular heights and at different pitches—in a word, it's dangerous. The handrails: thick bittersweet vines that stretch beyond the top step and encircle a Victorian hall mirror in the narrow space between the two guest rooms.

The Winter House's courtyard blends into the garden, with a few fanciful, colorful plantings and an ample terrace dedicated for relaxing, sheltered on two sides by the house itself and hemmed in on the other two sides by a wooden fence with a Chinese Chippendale pattern. The fence is planted with bright yellow variegated *Euonymus japonicus* and, at one time, bluish Irish junipers tied together to form imposing arches, now long since gone. A large Southern magnolia, previously espaliered against one of the house's walls, now towers above the paved terrace, which sports two large box balls and a rose that has overgrown its delicate metal obelisk-shaped tuteur. And there is a rudimentary outdoor shower, barely used and open to the elements.

Around the corner, the Winter House's original ladder has been repurposed as a rose trellis. Painted bright yellow, the ladder provides stark contrast against the humble but proficient greenhouse that sits next to it, which can be accessed from here as well as from the bathroom inside the Winter House. Featuring a temperature-controlled heater and automated glass panels, it has vastly better ventilation than its subpar predecessor and is now used year-round as a growing facility. In the autumn, tropical plants in the garden are dug up and stored here, and in the winter, we start our seeds, with varying degrees of success—just as with any garden.

Dash settled on an open-plan scheme for the main living area in the Winter House, which was converted from a mid-nineteenth-century barn. The bed, made from trees and branches felled by Hurricane Gloria in 1985, is anchored on wheelbarrow wheels (Dash liked to joke that he put them on in case he felt like rolling down Sagg Main Street). He painted the four-panel screen in the mid-1970s.

A WANDERING EYE

BELOW

The wheel-away bench outside the Winter House is inscribed "Madoo June 8 1991," in honor of Dash's sixtieth birthday. The yellow factory ladder once provided access to the Winter House's guest rooms and now plays host to an 'Étoile de Hollande' climbing rose, a velvety specimen introduced in 1879.

OPPOSITE, FROM TOP

The dining area includes a table painted by Dash in green acrylics and accented with lines and doodles in black Sharpie pen. Dash also painted the armoire, featuring the flat bridge that used to span the pond by the Summer House. The spatter-dash floor is intentionally similar to the floors in the Summer House living quarters.

The entrance to the Winter House features a stair railing made by hand from Madoo branch prunings.

PRIVATE

OPPOSITE
The Winter House's terrace features 'Yellow Purissima' and 'White Emperor' tulips in bloom alongside a Chinese Chippendale fence. The Long Border and the Hornbeam Bower are visible through the fog in the distance.

ABOVE
A detail of the 'Étoile de Hollande' rose

LEFT
A hundred or so pots of paperwhites are grown in the greenhouse for Merry Madoo, our annual mid-December holiday market.

BELOW LEFT
In winter, the greenhouse is so packed with tender plants from the garden that it is hard to move around inside.

OPPOSITE
The rear façade and courtyard of the Winter House after a February snowfall

BELOW
Accessed both from outside and from a bathroom within the Winter House, Madoo's greenhouse was built in 2015, replacing an earlier iteration that had outlived its usefulness.

MADOO SAGGAPONNACK N Y 11962

The list of old wives' and husbands' tales goes on and on and proves nothing more than that there will be weather. And plenty of it. As the late poet James Schuyler nobly stated, "I'm just glad there is some."

Foolish but optimistic gardeners like me go into their little greenhouses and start sowing.

--R. D.

Neighbors

by Marilee Foster

Along the northwest border of our farm is Madoo. Before that, it was Bob Dash's place. And before that it was part of the Rogers homestead—just the barns, barns left by a farmer with no heirs. That is when the artists could come to Sagaponack. They found studios: a roof, swallows in the rafters, the stage of farmland, a grove of trees, and an unmanicured lawn. The water, the ditch rows, pheasants—paradise, plus a general store with a post office attached.

For much of the time we were neighbors, we were strangers. I think we both willed it this way. Part of being in the garden is being alone. Had we begun a friendship earlier, every time we'd have passed each other, we'd have had to pay the other notice. That would have been wearisome because we were so often on opposite sides of the weedy fence line. Our stance of invisibility allowed us privacy as we wrangled with our plots. I was turning an old pasture back to vegetable production. He was painting with plants as well as pigment, growing a new chapter in an old place. But one day, when Sagg was soaked in one of its impenetrable fogs, we met.

I'd gone out to check the peas and they looked great, bright lines of white flowers dripping with moisture. Little pods, mere emerald scrapes where the petals had already fallen, exquisite. However, beyond the peas was a sight even more astounding. In Bob's garden, the magnolias bloomed and the pinks—in contrast to the hazy air that framed them—glowed. They glowed, opaque and illumined, gaudy and gorgeous through a deeply muted visual field. I walked toward the show, then awed, I stopped. I turned slowly to the west, where more, smaller magnolias were set in a haze of yellow and cream. It was then we saw each other. Bob and I stood, shoulder to shoulder, taking in the same thing from only slightly different vantage points.

I love Madoo because for all the time I have spent in this small corner of the world, I can get lost there, lose track of the sun, disoriented in the layout of the place. Madoo is never the same for long and yet it stays as a somewhat permanent fixture of an artist's love of the land and his commitment to its longevity.

Marilee Foster is a sixth-generation farmer based in Sagaponack, New York.

ABOVE
Robert Dash, *Sagaponack* (1980; serigraph, 27 x 38 inches). A view looking southward from Madoo, featuring the Foster farm barns under a violet sky in the early evening. [Credit: Gary J. Mamay]

RIGHT
The Foster farm, its meadow freshly mown, with a patch left uncut on purpose. The back side of Madoo's Long Border is to the right.

CHAPTER TEN

The Gazebo and the Frog Fountain

The water in the Frog Fountain is dyed black with organic food coloring, creating a mirrorlike effect. The bench to the left was designed and crafted at Madoo and mimics the curve of the path. A 'Zéphirine Drouhin' climbing rose and a pair of golden cypress standards thrive here.

When asked to explain the purple hue of the Gazebo, Dash was very fond of quoting Manet: "The very color of the atmosphere is violet." Indeed, in Dash's paintings where the skies melt into nothingness and the Gazebo disappears when the fog rolls in, violet is the color of the atmosphere. Although in truth, the structure itself is a few different shades of lavender, purples, and mauves, depending on whatever could be found in the painter's closet.

Aside from its arresting color, the Gazebo is notable for its hexagonal shape, with a double roof and, like the Bridge, wooden hoops in its upper half, which frame the views looking outward from inside. In its early days, the folly stood out in the garden among tiny saplings and assorted Irish junipers, but it has since nestled into the landscape, shaded by a substantial Southern magnolia and cushioned by hydrangea bushes.

Recently, its rotted railing was replaced. Our carpenter consulted one of Dash's books on Asian architecture and settled on a rectangular pattern that he then adapted to fit the spaces between the posts. The flooring also needed an upgrade, so the previously straight decking was changed to a hexagonal pattern, with each piece of wood sawn individually and carefully fit into place, since each side of the Gazebo is a different size.

Furnished with a hexagonal table and six matching stools, the Gazebo can be used as a spot for a casual lunch, a late-afternoon tea, or any leisurely occasion during which the subtly framed vistas of the garden can be savored. By late summer, the hydrangeas and shrubby clematis have crept their way into the space, nature taking over.

Lying in the shadow of the Gazebo and accessed via the Ginkgo Grove, the Frog Fountain is among the most recently renovated sections of Madoo. One approaches it from a curvy, narrow cobblestone path that wends past a grouping of limbed-up *Taxus* and Madoo's impressive tulip tree. Practically underfoot at this juncture rest the remains of the brick foundation of a milking house that was affixed to the old Loo building and became Dash's sleeping quarters during his first summer at Madoo. The fountain sits a few steps beyond, a simple concrete column topped by a sculpted frog spouting a stream of water.

Dash created this area of Madoo to honor his friend and art dealer Elaine Benson, who owned a namesake gallery in the nearby hamlet of Bridgehampton. The design scheme—currently including sulfur-flowered epimediums and variegated *Acorus*—is meant to evoke Benson's bottle-blond hair. Five golden cypress topiary standards, brought back to life from the Quincunx Gardens and replanted here, inject a jolt of chartreuse to the fountain and partially obscure it from the rest of the garden, while adding a playful edge.

A pollarded sycamore softly shades the area from overhead. In 2014, as part of a major renovation of the garden, this sycamore—then fully branched out—came under scrutiny, since the directive was to remove dead trees and prune others to let in more

MADOO SAGGAPONNACK N Y 11962

A certain purple I mixed, one much barded with rose and cinder, became soft and hazy, very much like those grays beloved of landscape painters.

--R. D.

light. Its branches reached from the Frog Fountain to the privet at the property line and, in the other direction, nearly to the edge of the Gazebo. Closer examination revealed that the tree had previously been pollarded, so out came the garden saws and in came the shafts of sunlight. Dash had planted a variegated *Ilex* at the foot of the tree (which is now pollarded every other year), and it has grown in such a way that it almost appears to be a green-and-cream hoopskirt around the tree's trunk. The *Ilex*'s bronze-y pink new growth is matched to a rose, 'Zéphirine Drouhin', that had suffered in the darkness for years before it was woven into the *Ilex* itself to protect it from deer. The rose now regularly sprouts from the *Ilex*, and the gardeners have trained its canes into garlands that adorn the floating globes of golden cypress.

The area's large-scale renovation was predicated by the poor condition of the bricks facing the fountain's water basin. After the bricks were removed, we decided that the concrete basin's shell was in good condition, so we stuccoed it in a cement color similar to that of the column. The electrical wires are buried beneath the pathway, and organic food dye is used to make the water black and appear like a mirror.

Even after Madoo's deciduous plants and trees lose their leaves and the garden is at its barest, the Gazebo and the Frog Fountain and their immediate surroundings hold up. The mottled sycamore trunk is just as majestic, and the golden cypress topiaries look like lollipops, echoing the Gazebo's bentwood rondels. Certain other shrubs and spring-blooming flowers ensure continuity in different seasons, and as spring unfurls, large daffodils traverse the area, replaced in the summer by various blue and white hydrangeas. These disparate plants and trees are tethered by a discrete curving boxwood hedge, behind which large clumps of *Amsonia hubrichtii* stretch their feathery leaves, providing a soft counterpoint and further underscoring the unexpectedly harmonious scheme.

BELOW

In midsummer, gold variegated foliage and faux bois pots planted with *Heuchera villosa* 'Palace Purple' flank the entrance to the Gazebo, which features a double roof and seven circular bentwood window frames.

RIGHT

A view of the Summer Lawn from the Gazebo. In mid-October, the *Amsonia hubrechtii* turns glorious gold.

LEFT

The faux bois pots at the entrance to the Gazebo put on a springtime show of 'Pretty Princess' tulips and purple sweet alyssum. [Credit: Timothy Heslop]

Spanish bluebells *(Hyacinthoides hispanica)* carpet the ground outside the Gazebo.

MADOO SAGGAPONNACK N Y 11962

I don't know whether I have been right or not, there being no truly unbreakable rules in gardening. As in painting, one manipulates a very few rather general, unspecific concepts or procedures and does not hew to an orderly list of commandments.

--R. D.

OPPOSITE
Five golden cypresses (*Chamaecyparis pisifera* 'Aurea'), transplanted from the Quincunx Gardens and punctuated with clumps of 'Tête-à-Tête' daffodils, surround the Frog Fountain.

LEFT
A detail of the 'Zéphirine Drouhin' rose, which is trained between the cypress standards

ABOVE
Taxus, their trunks crisscrossed with twine to deter rutting deer, line the path between the Frog Fountain and the Winter House lawn.

CHAPTER ELEVEN

The Summer Lawn

OPPOSITE
The Summer Lawn enjoys a majestic view of a *Magnolia grandiflora* 'Bracken's Brown Beauty', which dwarfs the Gazebo, and a whimsical arbor with barn doors that can be closed.

RIGHT
The Summer Lawn, seen from beneath the weeping privet in early spring. Scattered clumps of daffodils pop up through the grass.

Lawn space is relatively limited at Madoo, and if Dash had his way, there would probably be even less of it today. In such a densely planted garden, a bit of open sky is a necessity, and the Summer Lawn offers the opportunity for a respite, not to mention a staging area for a variety of events held to raise money for the nonprofit Madoo Conservancy. In the far corner, two Dash-designed Adirondack chairs—currently painted yellow and pink—offer an inviting perch for taking in the garden, including an impressive stretch of roses *sur chaîne*, a weeping English oak tree, the Gazebo, and the giant tulip tree.

Similar in style to those at Wave Hill garden in the Bronx and reminiscent of Gerrit Rietveld's famous *Red Blue Chair*, Madoo's Adirondacks differ in one important way: Their armrests are extra wide, the better to accommodate cocktails, Dash proclaimed. Steeply pitched, their seats make people look up and out, whether they're drinking or not.

The roses *sur chaîne* comprise a mix of climbers in red and pink tones, originally planted at the base of 9-foot-tall posts capped by finials. Their canes were then trained onto chains draped between each post. In mid-June, there is an explosion of blooms, although the entire length isn't in flower at once, thanks to a variety of specimens ranging from 'New Dawn' to 'Florentina' and even two *rubiginosa* shrub roses.

Meadow plants, courtesy of both the gardeners and Mother Nature, peek through the rose wall and add a bit of froth to all the reds and pinks. *Daucus carota* 'Dara', bronze fennel, *Digitalis purpurea*, and *Scabiosa*, among a variety of other perennials, contribute to the show until the rose bloom is over, after which they sort of disappear into the background of deep green privet that unifies this portion of the Summer Lawn.

Two brick walkways between the roses and the privet meet in a corner punctuated by a large vintage terra-cotta urn. The eastern walkway is additionally graced with a laburnum arbor inspired by Rosemary Verey's legendary one at Barnsley House in Gloucestershire and anchored with posts sheathed in garters of 'Manhattan' euonymus. Laburnums do not fare well on eastern Long Island, and several of the original plantings have died over the years—as they did at Verey's arbor, which eventually needed to be replaced.

Midway through the laburnum arbor lies another rondel, this one anchored by a makeshift fountain nestled in a foundation of tattered brick and cement pavers—rather treacherous to anyone wearing stilettos. Vaguely suggesting English Arts and Crafts, the terra-cotta-toned aggregate column is topped with a cement fleur-de-lis, which spouts a trickle of water that slowly makes its way down the column to a small underground cistern below.

MADOO SAGGAPONNACK N Y 11962

A story of stubbornness and friendship, the arbor was put in because I was told that it was impossible to grow laburnum due to our salt-laden gales, laburnum being utterly intolerant of winds from the sea. . . . On a cold November day, the great, missed Rosemary Verey visited the garden for the first time. "And this," I said innocently, vaingloriously, ignorantly, "is my laburnum arbor." I recall her slightly mocking smile. Her first missile of thanks: a postcard of her famous arbor at Barnsley House. I wired her on the inst. "You certainly know how to hurt a guy." Rosemary telephoned. "It was merely the first card at hand," she said.

--R. D.

OPPOSITE
The laburnum arbor, inspired by Rosemary Verey's at Barnsley House in Gloucestershire and planted in the mid-1980s. The trees have outgrown the confines of the arbor, which is slated for renovation.

LEFT
Lilacs have been trained over the top of the arbor and a path leading to the Summer Lawn. [Credit: Alejandro Saralegui]

BELOW LEFT
Iris germanica 'Indian Chief' was hybridized in 1929. At Madoo, it grows under the roses *sur chaîne*.

BELOW
'American Pillar' roses are trained up a post and extended on either side on chains to successive posts, forming the roses *sur chaîne* feature that lines two sides of the Summer Lawn.

The Summer Lawn offers a sweeping view of garden layers, from 'Golden Splendor' lilies to a thick stand of *Thalictrum* 'Elin' and a towering tulip tree.

BELOW
A rare weeping privet, *Ligustrum vulgare* 'Pendulum', blooms in the Summer Lawn in late June, with the Magnolia Bosque as a backdrop. [Credit: Alejandro Saralegui]

ABOVE
An afternoon fog rolling in from the Atlantic Ocean provides a moody setting for a majestic, rare weeping English oak, *Quercus robur* 'Pendula', which Dash bought for $35 in 2012 and planted as a small 1-gallon sapling. [Credit: Kendell Cronstrom]

LEFT
The view of the Summer Lawn after a light dusting of snow in the winter

LEFT
A pair of Adirondack chairs designed by Dash sit in a corner of the Summer Lawn, framed by wispy bronze fennel.

BELOW LEFT
Surprisingly hardy, a South African river lily (*Hesperantha coccinea* 'Zeal Salmon') peeks from behind the Summer Lawn fence.

OPPOSITE
Swags of an unidentified climbing rose and 'Jasmina' and 'Florentina' roses make up the bulk of Madoo's roses *sur chaîne* feature.

BELOW
Chrysanthemum 'Hillside Sheffield Pink', with its lovely single flowers and bright yellow eye, mirrors the simplicity of the fence.

MADOO SAGGAPONNACK N Y 11962

An infliction and not a comfort, [the Adirondack chair] is most adept at holding wet and soggy leaves, is impossible to rise from gracefully, and gives all sitters a deep, rather stubborn, look, with knees against faces when seen head-on. Its only function, it seems to me, is to get into a lot of plein air American painting, because it has come to be entirely emblematic of summer. Only John Calvin would approve.

--R. D.

CHAPTER TWELVE

The Magnolia Bosque and the Hermit's Hut

The outer edge of the Magnolia Bosque is heavily planted, providing a sense of privacy from inside. Here, a yellow honeysuckle is trained on a post and blooms behind a medley of bishop's-weed, goatsbeard, and *Veronicastrum virginicum* 'Album', as well as 'Mount Everest' alliums.

About a year before his death, Dash surveyed an entangled web of magnolias at Madoo and proclaimed, "Those trees are big enough now. Let's remove the other plants around them and let visitors see their differences up close." And so, the Magnolia Bosque was born—although not quickly, as the clearing took place over the course of the following two years.

The location of the bosque, centered between the Summer Lawn and the Summer House, was for years a barely tended mass of grasses and shrubs—Dash was an early adapter to native plants and meadows. He later added a ring of *Taxus* around the perimeter, spaced every 10 feet or so. Then came the magnolias—planted as saplings, like virtually every other tree at Madoo. These and the *Taxus* roughly formed a circle with a space in the middle, which was largely given over to the grasses before the clearing took place.

The Magnolia Bosque features nine varieties of magnolia, a few of whose names have been lost. There are several *Magnolia* × *soulangeana* and a dark *M. liliiflora* that reblooms in late summer. One is certainly a *M. wilsonii*, one a late-blooming *M. macrophylla*, one a *M. denudata*, one a *M.* 'Elizabeth', and yet another a crazy mystery that has one trunk with pale white-and-pink flowers and another in a darker color closer to raspberry. A possible explanation for the latter: Dash planted two trees in the same hole, and their trunks fused together as they grew.

In addition to the bosque, magnolias pop up in profusion elsewhere at Madoo, including several *M. stellata*, which begin unfurling their petals one after another in a great big explosion of pink and white in advance of the creamy yellow of the later-blooming 'Elizabeth' and the perfumed crescendo in the bosque itself. So far, the magnolias have charted an uneven and compelling course. A prime specimen whose branches shaped the bosque's center started to give up the ghost limb by limb, so we cut it down and left its trunk at about 3 feet. Lo and behold, it sent up shoots from the base and sides the following spring. When it flowers in a few years, we hope to determine which variety it is. The *M. wilsonii*, too, is losing its limbs, caused by accidental damage and scarred bark from rutting deer. It is already sending up suckers, which we will leave and allow to evolve into new trunks.

An outlier thrives within the bosque, a testament to Madoo's quirky nature. A *Franklinia alatamaha*, it has lovely lemon-scented camellia-like flowers that carpet the lawn from the second half of August well into October. The specimen tree, discovered by botanists John Bartram and his son William on the banks of Georgia's Altamaha River in 1765 (the same year that the elder Bartram was named the "King's botanist" for North America), it was propagated at their Philadelphia nursery and essentially saved from extinction, as there have been no *Franklinia* sightings in the wild since 1803.

Just beyond the *Franklinia* lies the Hermit's Hut, originally the site of a small shed that Dash established here, riffing on a common feature found on eighteenth-century English

MADOO SAGGAPONNACK N Y 11962

A package from Wayside at the post office when I went for the second mail. *Rosa* [*banksiae*] 'Lutea' entirely in leaf, so will keep it in its pot indoors until roses outside are in large leaf. And a *Franklinia*, a small tree far too tender for our climate, but I think I have a pocket as protected from the prevailing winds as if a high stone wall had been built there.

--R. D.

RIGHT
At least nine varieties of magnolias grow in the bosque, including *Magnolia* 'Elizabeth', celebrated for its yellow blossoms and the first of its kind to be developed by the Brooklyn Botanic Garden, which patented it in 1977.

OPPOSITE
Industrial designer Marc Newson's *Lathed Table*, fabricated from a single piece of Bardiglio marble and surrounded by a suite of Fermob chairs, beckons from the center of the Magnolia Bosque. It's a dreamy setting for alfresco lunches and dinners.

estates. (He often joked that he considered hiring a hermit to occupy it.) Studded with several 'Paul's Himalayan Musk' rambling roses, the hut's wood eventually rotted and was replaced by a domed arbor made of plastic and metal plumbing pipes. There's still no hermit in residence, but the roses and their millions of lightly scented pink flowers are a wonder, especially when appreciated from inside the "hut."

Not to be outdone by the impressive rambling roses, a remarkable weeping privet offers contrast and a rounded shape that grounds all the bosque magnolias when viewed from the Summer Lawn. Erupting in white blossoms in late June, the entire shrub is a sight to behold. Interestingly, people only seem to ask about it when they view its leafless back side from within the Magnolia Bosque, curious about the tree with the sculptural branches.

To mark Madoo's twenty-fifth anniversary as a public garden, a swath of plants in silvery tones was designated for an area formerly occupied by limbed-up highbush blueberries. The hedging here is the wonderful *Salix purpurea* 'Canyon Blue', sheared to about the same height as nearby boxwood plantings and a wonderful complement to silver-leaved plants with flowers in pale lavenders, blues, and pinks, including *Stachys byzantina*, *Silene coronaria*, and *Echinacea pallida*.

Standing at the very center of the Magnolia Bosque is perhaps its most defining feature: a large dining table that was gifted to Madoo and now serves as the locale of many a festive occasion on warm summer evenings. The table, a 1-ton hand-lathed piece of Bardiglio marble by the Australian industrial designer Marc Newson, perches on a circle of crushed granite, the perfect complement to a circular treasury of trees and shrubs.

Just across from the entrance to the Magnolia Bosque is an aging crab apple tree with whirling dervish-like branches. To the right, a multistemmed *Franklinia alatamaha* shades the path and mounded *Ilex glabra* shrubs.

BELOW

Lamb's ear (*Stachys byzantina*) and Spanish bluebells (*Hyacinthoides hispanica*)

RIGHT COLUMN, FROM TOP

The Magnolia Bosque is underplanted with Spanish bluebells in midspring.

The *Franklinia alatamaha* starts blooming in late August and continues into October.

OPPOSITE

The Hermit's Hut is a makeshift arbor for three 'Paul's Himalayan Musk' rambling roses. The entrance path is detailed in brick and telephone pole pavers.

MADOO SAGGAPONNACK N Y 11962

The Hermit's Hut still lacks a hermit, although duties are slight. . . . He (or she) sits there looking quite dour and makes barely audible but clearly derisive comments about the passing visitors. The hermit gets a gallon of beer a day and a loaf of bread. Saturdays, we hose the hermit down. Although I have added the amelioration of warm water to the hose, we have yet to have any takers.

--R. D.

ABOVE
In bloom, the 'Paul's Himalayan Musk' roses smother the Hermit's Hut and scent the air with their light fragrance.

OPPOSITE
Detail of the 'Paul's Himalayan Musk' roses

CHAPTER THIRTEEN

The Potager and the Potager Terrace

By late summer, the Potager is teeming with vegetables and herbs. Purple loosestrife, kept in check, plays foil to 'Grandpa Ott' morning glories on the hoops.

During Dash's first summer at Madoo, when he was virtually camping on the land, a local farmer took pity on the scrawny city boy and gave him tomatoes to supplant his meager diet. As he concentrated on his painting while also planning his house to be, Dash must have thought of planting a vegetable garden—perhaps just tomatoes, radishes, and lettuces grown from seed purchased at the local hardware store, the kind of produce he had grown as a boy at his family's summer retreat in Tuxedo Park. Such simplicity was likely perfect in his mind, until he fell under the spell of Rosemary Verey years later and learned of her kitchen garden at Barnsley House. Verey had come to prominence in the 1970s alongside British gardening gurus including Penelope Hobhouse and Beth Chatto, who were bringing back the glory days of horticulture—albeit without an army of help, as in the Edwardian era.

Verey had assiduously studied decorative eighteenth-century French vegetable and flower gardens called potagers, elaborate in design compared with their earliest iterations, which were intended primarily for making soup (or potage) for aristocrats and peasants alike. Jean-Baptiste de La Quintinie, a seventeenth-century French lawyer, elevated the humble potager to an art form when he created *le Potager du Roi* for King Louis XIV at Versailles, although today's versions can range from basic—perhaps rows of vegetables with an occasional flowering plant like calendula, to ward off disease or insects—to complex, such as the grand boxwood-edged color-coordinated parterres of Villandry.

Madoo, defying logic, has no easy-access door from the Summer House kitchen to its 26-by-52-foot plot. The plan of the garden mirrors Verey's own potager, but simplified and scaled down. (A photocopy of the potager at Barnsley House still exists, with a few recommendations scribbled down in Verey's hand for Dash to follow.) Box-edged beds and narrow paths made of garden pavers from the local stone yard were certainly innovative for the time during which the Potager was established. Tulips filled the center beds, blooming in the spring and underpinned with red-tinted salad greens, and other quadrants featured everything from peppers to cabbages. Originally, the Potager was demarcated by a post-and-beam fence and a rustic metal gate, but today it's reined in by a step-over wattle fence, made from black bamboo and cedar stakes and replenished yearly by our carpenter.

Dash hadn't taken into account the competitive nature of boxwood roots, which starved the vegetables of water and sustenance. He eventually removed the boxwood and transplanted it to the Long Border, gaining larger vegetable beds in the process, but he grew tired of planning and caring for the Potager and experimented with lower-maintenance fruiting shrubs, intending to make preserves for the long East End winters. Toward the end of his life, he once again switched things up, settling on a limited, mostly ornamental palette of vegetables.

MADOO SAGGAPONNACK N Y 11962

Originally, the Potager was one large collapsed cross of brick and chives. The segments outside this pattern were planted in triangles and squares of vegetables and flowers. Well and good, but clipping the chives back after flowering (they will do this twice) became a messy, oozing, smelly chore. Jeans, shoes, fingers, knees reeked of chives. So too the secateurs. Chive juice got into my hair as well.

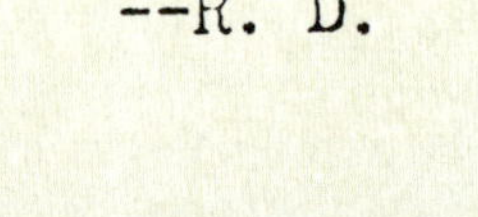

--R. D.

ABOVE
The center circle of the Potager is planted in 'Banja Luka' tulips, a yellow Darwin hybrid that is feathered with bright red and appears orangish from afar. The hoops in the middle slyly nod to the topiaried holly along the perimeter.

OPPOSITE
On the Potager's side beds, 'Chicago Hardy' fig standards underplanted with nasturtiums frame the central circle, planted here with potatoes and shishito peppers. Three Claverton cloches, made in England, are used to protect seedlings from cold weather and rabbits in early spring, and to start hardy lettuces and spinaches in the fall.

Today the Potager produces vegetables and fruits that are harvested once and keep well. The season starts in the autumn, with a saffron haul courtesy of *Crocus sativus*'s violet-blue flowers: Perfect for risottos and paellas, a little goes a long way. Then comes the planting of the best of the previous crop of garlic cloves, ensuring even larger tasty heads of the allium the following summer. (Dash planted garlic not just in the Potager but elsewhere at Madoo, which we leave in situ for its decorative curly scapes in June.) In early December, the gardeners plant about 400 tulip bulbs in the center, typically one large-blossomed variety like 'Menton' or 'Dordogne' or 'Banja Luka', for a knock-your-socks-off show the following May.

After the tulips are pulled, several varieties of potatoes are planted in the central bed, at about the same time neighboring farmers are planting theirs: Fingerlings and Russian banana types are current favorites. Once these are harvested, the small orange chestnut-flavored Japanese squash known as potimarron or red kuri takes their place. Occasionally, we plant 'Speckled Hound', a beautiful pumpkin squash reminiscent of Cinderella's carriage, with dusty orange-hued skin and sage-colored markings. It's an ideal choice for Julia Child's signature pumpkin soup, baked in the actual shell of the pumpkin.

Other beds in the potager produce a revolving crop of vegetables. Tomatoes, started from seed in the greenhouse, include 'Gold Medal', notable for its orange-and-yellow-streaked skin and apricot-colored flesh. Peppers of all sorts—Dash loved them—proliferate, while an eye is simultaneously kept on making sure

ABOVE
The Potager Terrace features potted succulents and a sitting area anchored by an Indian howdah originally used for riding elephants. The upright boxwoods in the foreground are 'Graham Blandy'.

ABOVE RIGHT
'Chioggia' beets dry in the sun after being harvested and washed. [Credit: Alejandro Saralegui]

RIGHT
Harvested garlic dries in the potting shed. [Credit: Alejandro Saralegui]

the plants don't get out of hand. We still don't know what to do with the cardoons, but their bold foliage is extraordinary. If you have the patience to blanch them five times and then gratinée them with aged Gruyère cheese, they're delicious.

One feature of the Potager, a strict departure from Dash's time, is a "hidden nursery" in the back, partly obscured by a brightly painted trellis on the adjacent Potager Terrace. Here, dahlias grow in profusion and provide endless pleasure in cut-flower arrangements, although Dash did not believe in cutting gardens and would shudder at the thought. (If you spied a flower inside a vase in the house, it was because its stem had snapped. More likely, one would see fresh asparagus fronds stuffed into a pewter chalice on the dining table or a few autumn crocus bulbs scattered on a shelf and miraculously blooming without soil or water.)

The masses of dahlias, grown in rows of riotous color, draw inspiration from

Britain-based gardener Charlie McCormick's dahlia beds at his former garden in West Dorset. The tubers are planted in the warm ground around Memorial Day weekend, then dug up after the first frost, cleaned, and stored in milk crates in Madoo's unheated basement. Not included among them: extra-large or

MADOO SAGGAPONNACK N Y 11962

What vegetables I planted were selected for architectural worth, so that balloons of second-year leek flowers swayed above red and yellow chard and, in other sections, precise little rondeaux of little-leaf basil pressed against pepper bushes in red, yellow, and chocolate fruit, all enclosed in tightly clipped, low English box. Tulips and lettuces make a delightful combination.

--R. D.

dinner-plate dahlias, which prove to be very difficult to arrange in a vase.

The Potager Terrace once served as the location of the kennel for Dash's dogs, including the first Barnsley and his successors. (Dash had three Norwich terriers over a period of about thirty years, all named Barnsley.) A simple fenced-in space with a beach-pebble ground, it was planted with spare topiaries here and there, including a now-gone triumphal hawthorn arch that marked the entrance. The kennel was eventually dispensed with and the area laid with cement garden pavers dotted with pots and bits of furniture, including a vintage howdah. Dash loved to sit on the howdah during the spring, admiring his seedlings and newly purchased plants and contemplating where they would go in the garden. Some never left the terrace, as he would often instruct the gardeners to remove a paver and plant a shrub or tree in its place.

A wisteria, trained as a standard, spirals skyward out of the paving, and antique French metal étagères display Victorian glass cloches, often accompanied by pots of flowering and scented pelargoniums. Most recently, two strips of pavers on either side of the terrace were removed, their hollows planted with *Lysimachia nummularia* 'Aurea' and *Allium* 'Blue Curls'. Despite the odds, these thrive in the stony soil, encouraged by the heat from the sunbaked pavers.

OPPOSITE
Buds of edible cardoons resemble artichokes. At Madoo the plants are grown mainly for their dramatic gray-green foliage.

CLOCKWISE FROM TOP LEFT
The dark stems of a self-seeded *Angelica atropurpurea* contrast with their nectar-rich lime-green flowers.

'Gold Medal' tomatoes, hard to find at most farm stands on the East End, are grown at Madoo for their delicious flavor and rich color.

Trimming garlic scapes increases the size of the garlic bulbs underground. Here the scapes are gathered in a trug made by UK-based artist Jane Crisp. [Credit: Alejandro Saralegui]

A fruiting 'Chicago Hardy' fig

ABOVE
Before they unfurl, the 'Banja Luka' tulips—named after a city in Bosnia and Herzegovina—are rather demure. The full blooms can reach almost 6 inches in diameter.

OPPOSITE
This happy clump of *Inula helenium* has been blooming at Madoo for decades without any care or attention. The plant was known in ancient Greek and Roman times for its medicinal qualities and more recently as a flavoring for absinthe.

Dahlias grow in an area of the Potager previously used by Dash as a nursery bed, hemmed in by *Taxus* on one side and privet on another. Everything reaches its apogee by late summer, when the white garlic chives are in bloom and the figs are ripening.

OPPOSITE
The crab apple tree across from the Potager Terrace is on its last legs, but a pink clematis hasn't given up on it.

RIGHT
The Potager is fenced with wattle made from black bamboo. In the spring, daffodils planted in Dash's time appear everywhere.

BELOW RIGHT
An allium bursts into bloom, in tandem with the feathery new growth of bronze fennel.

LEFT
A bronze turtle sits atop a cast-stone column.

LEFT
'Tartan', an extraordinary dinner plate dahlia, is an exception to varieties that have been chosen mostly to accommodate cut-flower arrangements.

BELOW LEFT
Included in the dahlia beds is 'Honka Black', a single variety beloved by bees and other pollinators.

BELOW
'Princess Nadine', an anemone-type dahlia, fights for attention alongside a similarly hued ball-type dahlia called 'Safe Shot'.

OPPOSITE
An errant monkshood, dating from Dash's time, pokes through the dahlias.

OPPOSITE
Outside the entrance to the Potager, a tree peony planted by Dash is set off by *Geum* 'Totally Tangerine'.

ABOVE
Fritillaria meleagris, more commonly known as snake's head fritillary or guinea-hen flower, is a natural at Madoo, where the neighboring farm's guinea fowl often pay a visit.

On the walkway adjacent to the Potager and the Potager Terrace, an unidentified large-leaf holly has been pruned to have "wedding cake" tiers, exposing bits of the trunk's mottled gray bark.

BELOW

The Potager Terrace looking shipshape after its hedges and topiaries have been sheared. A potted sunset-hued paddle plant, *Kalanchoe luciae*, at waist level in a vintage stand, echoes the color of the red cement pavers. [Credit: Kendell Cronstrom]

RIGHT

By mid-November, the Potager has been cleaned for the winter. The fig standards are protected in makeshift cages filled with leaves, which are transferred to the compost pile in the spring.

BELOW RIGHT

The hips of the 'Aloha' rose provide winter interest.

OPPOSITE

Boltonia asteroides and *Clematis virginiana* billow beyond a keyhole opening in the trellised "shed" attached to the south end of the Summer House.

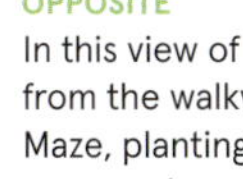

OPPOSITE
In this view of the Potager from the walkway to the Maze, plantings include joe-pye weed, purple loosestrife, *Boltonia asteroides*, and asparagus. [Credit: Kendell Cronstrom]

LEFT
Backed by a blue treillage panel, a French plant étagère holds pots, glass cloches, and vintage watering cans.

BELOW LEFT
These snowdrops, dug up from the berm near the Winter House, were temporarily housed in a clay pot before being replanted.

BELOW
A few years ago, a post painted to match the Summer House was added to a corner of the Potager Terrace, allowing this 'Aloha' rose to flourish.

ABOVE
Large-scale, tulip-like autumn crocuses pop up all over Madoo.

OPPOSITE
Perennial sunflowers (*Helianthus* × *multiflorus*) spill over the blue treillage panel.

A Jack of All Trades Who Was Master of Most

by Robert Storr

OPPOSITE
Robert Dash, *The Window* (1964; acrylic on panel, 10 x 8 inches). Dash painted this work in the Southampton house of artist Fairfield Porter, a longtime friend. [Credit: Gary J. Mamay]

Robert Dash was blessed—or cursed, depending on your view of specialization being an essential criterion of seriousness—by an embarrassment of talents. In truth, almost nothing, not even what would embarrass most people, could cramp his style. His was not just a quick study of those capacities—in fact, he never went to art school or, for that matter, "gardening school." To the contrary, he possessed an expansive mind and creative sensibility, and an uncanny ability to find his own way of doing just about anything and everything that interested him. And many things did, deeply.

As a student, he edited the literary journal of the University of New Mexico, for which he solicited contributions from an array of prominent American painters and poets, plus Rufino Tamayo, a renowned Mexican artist who provided a drawing for its cover. While in that role, he was drawn into the New York School poetry scene at the height of its flowering and was befriended by John Ashbery, James Schuyler, and Frank O'Hara, whose typescripts hung on his walls. Invited to make a Hollywood screen test with Bette Davis, he could mimic just about any star of the stage or cinema and took the greatest delight in over-the-top renditions of them, particularly Dame Edith Evans in Oscar Wilde's *The Importance of Being Earnest* (a character flaw of which he was never guilty). A classical pianist in his youth, he hosted piano competitions at Madoo during his later life. He was also a stylish writer, of both poetry and prose, for many years penning a garden column for the *East Hampton Star*. And he was a much-in-demand lecturer with a notoriously naughty "way with words."

But these multiple forays into other avocations will never obscure his highly regarded reputation as a visual artist as well as the creator of Madoo, one of the lushest, most idiosyncratically metamorphic gardens to be found in North America. He was justly famous for the latter, both throughout the Western Hemisphere and in Europe—especially in England, where his friends and regular houseguests Rosemary Verey and Penelope Hobhouse ruled the horticultural world. Yet it was as a visual artist that he first made his name, and his oeuvre provides the backbone of his other creative pursuits.

Upon returning from the Southwest in the 1950s, Dash plunged into the ferment of downtown Manhattan during Abstract Expressionism's most fecund period. His entrée was having focused attention on the tendency's leading lights, chief among them Willem de Kooning, who lived with his wife, Elaine, in Springs, only a short distance as the crow flies from Dash's home in Sagaponack. Also important to Bob's development as a painter was Fairfield Porter, who provided him with the tools to forge his own path as an artist. Porter was never any more of an abstract painter than Bob was and still less of an expressionist, but he was a stunningly deft gestural realist in an unselfconsciously

ABOVE
Robert Dash, *Dining, Spring* (1972; acrylic on linen, 24 x 24 inches). An early depiction of the dining area in the Summer House. More than fifty years later, the furniture remains the same, but the farm view is now totally obscured. [Credit: Gary J. Mamay]

OPPOSITE
Robert Dash, *Dwarf Pear Flowering* (1971–72; acrylic on linen, 70 x 50 inches). This tree once grew next to a wall of the Summer House. [Credit: Gary J. Mamay]

decorative mode premised on improvisatory brushwork and subtly modulated tonal color. For Dash, Porter set both an unimpeachable modern art precedent and a rationale for a fresh but hardly rebellious idiom and subject matter, to which the younger artist brought his own distinctive panache.

In keeping with the model set by Porter, Bob Dash limned pictures of his immediate environs—the rooms of his house, a coiling structure pieced together from existing farm buildings—while keenly monitoring the seasons of his garden both enclosed by the residence and extending outward to his rail-fenced property line and the potato fields, and even more fields and waterways unfolding beyond them. The enlivening impact of these close encounters with reality is evident in all of Dash's early- and middle-period interiors, and landscapes regardless of how far they stray from traditionally meticulous naturalism. One can regard his paintings, drawings, and prints as a comprehensive survey and inventory of natural and man-made sights that quite literally constituted his everyday "surround," which cut to the quick of how something familiar can suddenly come across as "fresh" in the hands of a skilled and discriminating artist, even when you can plainly recognize its antecedents. Because all flowers are not alike, nor are all trees.

Robert Storr is an artist, curator, and former Dean of Fine Arts at Yale University.

CHAPTER FOURTEEN

The Maze, the Sunken Terrace, and the Yellow Arch

OPPOSITE
The contorted mulberries hold their leaves well into November. In midsummer, when they get too dense, the trees are gently pruned to let more light into the Maze.

RIGHT
Before being pollarded in the winter, the mulberries have wildly expressive branches. After being cut, the branches are used as supports or cages for plants in the spring.

A row of privet, limbed and pruned by Dash to be almost startlingly unrecognizable, used to separate the Potager from the Maze. Rosemary Verey claimed that the privet's trunks looked like the knocked knees of aged ballerinas—and eventually they were retired, having dried out and lost their luster. Another planting opportunity presented itself. One season, we experimented with several varieties of sunflowers, which performed exuberantly, filling this stretch with bright color and whimsy for a too-short burst of time. Perennials and repeating annuals like *Inula*, *Verbena bonariensis*, *Clematis virginiana*, and purple loosestrife currently fill the gap.

By definition, the adjacent Maze doesn't quite live up to its name. Positioned next to the Potager and visible from the Summer House's guest room and bath, it's separated from the house by only a narrow planting bed and a concrete paver walkway—a passage so tight that it's nearly impossible not to brush against the Maze's *Taxus* hedge wall while walking alongside it. The entry is hardly inviting, if even findable: just two narrow slits of *Taxus* wide enough for a child of eight to slip through. And what's inside isn't really a maze, but a rather complicated piece of diagonal brickwork and topiaries, a foursquare design lacking clear delineation and muddled further by even smaller passages between each quad. A pollarded contorted mulberry (*Morus alba* 'Unryu') anchors each of the four squares. The pollarding makes the trees' leaves quite large, on branches that extend well beyond the allotted square footage, creating a lovely, if awkward, canopy each summer—thick enough that the gardeners often need to trim them back.

The tight planting pockets within the Maze's *Taxus* structure bear all sorts of flowers, both intentional and seeded by the wind. Delicate crocuses planted by Dash emerge in early spring, followed a bit later by pale green lady's mantle (*Alchemilla mollis*), water droplets dancing on their unfurling fuzzy foliage in advance of their showy chartreuse flowers. Tall lilies appear to pop out of the *Taxus*, their brilliant yellow flowers stretching toward the contorted mulberries overhead. By late summer, the blue perennial *Ageratum* and

MADOO SAGGAPONNACK N Y 11962

Which English maze it was that I got lost in while biblical rains made my jacket and trousers washcloths, I cannot recall. If only I had the wit and wisdom to bring some corn to establish a trail, or recalled that, in a maze, it is important to always turn left. Or is it right? "Got stuck, did you?" asked the sympathetic pub keeper where I had repaired for a warming shot or two. I vowed that, if I ever made a maze, it would be user-friendly and that one could easily see egress before one entered.

--R. D.

RIGHT
Contorted mulberries (*Morus alba* 'Unryu') grow in each quadrant of the *Taxus*-hedged Maze. The painted mahogany railings, a gift from a contractor, were placed precisely where Dash had installed a simple spindle railing that had rotted away.

OPPOSITE
A pair of *Magnolia* × *soulangeana* bloom over the Sunken Terrace.

the burgundy-leaved shiso (*Perilla frutescens*) provide unexpected, unconventional contrast.

Abutting the Maze on its northern edge is the Sunken Terrace, an early feature of Madoo. Accessed by two small steps downward, it's not truly sunken, but the name is evocative and has managed to stick. A variety of magnolias and a large moss cedar (*Juniperus chinensis*) surround an expansive patio lined with brick and surrounded by a border of concrete pavers. The patterned brick, delightful to behold on its own, is amplified by a custom brick carpet, designed by artist Margaret Kerr and gifted to Madoo in 2019. Transferred in three sections from Kerr's Springs studio and inlaid within the Sunken Terrace's existing brick basket weave, the 4-by-20-foot "runner" features a primary motif of Celtic knots bordered by a diamond pattern along its length and "fringe" on its short sides. Somewhat miraculously, the brick carpet lies perfectly flat in the Sunken Terrace at the exact level of the concrete pavers, accentuated by pale-toned beach stones that fill the gaps on all four sides.

Magnolia petals blanket the Sunken Terrace's floor in the spring, a delicious light fragrance emanating from the pink snowstorm. Over the years, the Sunken Terrace grew darker, with trees blocking almost all the light. A bit of judicious pruning and carefully considered transplantation opened up the area to new possibilities, as did the death of a neighbor's tree that shrouded its eastern flank, but what to do? A large bust of Beethoven, spray-painted gold and previously accentuated and illuminated by a large round mirror, was a showboat-y sore thumb desperately calling out for a new home. Some thought this plastic take on Antoine Bourdelle's scowling composer would be better off in a dumpster, but it speaks to Dash's lifelong interest in music and his early education as a classical pianist. A discreet spot was found where some privet had been cleared at the Sunken Terrace's northern end, and today the musician casts a stern watch from a simple brick plinth.

The largely green plant palette needed a boost to attract guests, although the red brick, magnolias, and abundant lush foliage already

LEFT
The Sunken Terrace's brick carpet was designed and made by Margaret Kerr, an artist who lived in nearby Springs. The artwork fits perfectly within the center of the paved terrace.

BELOW LEFT
Vintage zinc washtubs are hung on the Summer House wall opposite the Maze. At Madoo, they are used to clean vegetables or filled with ice to cool wine at events.

BELOW
At the entrance to the Sunken Terrace, *Aruncus dioicus* almost blocks the path completely.

MADOO SAGGAPONNACK N Y 11962

The perfume of the 'Casa Blanca' lily snaps the heart, wobbles the knees, is entirely addictive. Neither high nor low in the mist attic of odors, it is a middle scent, where cloves, bergamot, dianthus, and sassafras spin their strands.

--R. D.

suggested the genteel Southern courtyards common to Charleston and Savannah. A secondary planting layer was incorporated to create winter interest, as the Sunken Terrace lies close to the studio space where most of Madoo's winter programming takes place. Several varieties of *Hamamelis* and hellebores have been scattered about, making this area among the first to bloom, starting in February and continuing through April. Anchoring the Sunken Terrace itself, a double large planter is stuffed with tulip bulbs in November, producing a virtual lasagna of vibrantly colored early-, middle-, and late-spring tulips that take over once the winter flowers have had their moment. When the last of the tulips fade away, glossy green farfugiums replace them, having patiently waited their turn in the greenhouse all winter and spring.

To reach the Summer Studio, visitors follow a narrow corridor off the Sunken Terrace, passing under Madoo's iconic postmodern Yellow Arch midway. The structure, another Dash-invented folly, mimics a similarly arched yellow door that once provided access to the Summer House's guest quarters. The door floats about 6 inches above grade, with a mock "step" of *Buxus sinica* var. *insularis* 'Justin Brouwers' at its base. This slow-growing boxwood responds well to shearing and perfectly suits its purpose.

Extremely narrow boxwood hedges of two types line either side of the corridor, appearing the same from a distance but clearly different upon close inspection of their foliage. Lying parallel to the corridor's eastern hedge is a zigzag hedge made of *Taxus*, established in a dry area where few other plants have been successful. It's truly the right plant in the right place, although it required a fair amount of coddling before it took hold. More challenging is filling in the triangles created by the zigzag, although Dash's beloved 'Casa Blanca' lilies have done well here, sometimes rising to 8 feet, a startling statement matched only by Madoo's trademark Yellow Arch looming above them.

The Sunken Terrace's central double container, designed by architect Dale Booher for interior designer Charlotte Moss, has a layered springtime planting of tulips in purple, white, and pink tones, including 'Violet Beauty', 'White Elegance', 'Queen of the Night', 'Purple Dance', and 'Candy Club'.

BELOW
Naked ladies (*Lycoris squamigera*) seemingly pop out of nowhere in August. Their strap-like leaves actually come up in the spring but then die back, leaving their bulbs with enough energy to send up the naked flower stalk.

RIGHT
At the very beginning of spring, the *Cornus mas* comes into bloom while the hellebores are almost on their way out. The vintage French strap-metal settees have been at Madoo since the early 1970s.

OPPOSITE
In late May, after the tulips are spent, the double container is filled with leopard plant (*Farfugium japonicum*), which is potted up every autumn and stored in Madoo's greenhouse.

OPPOSITE
A stand of Turk's-cap lilies (*Lilium superbum*), native to the eastern United States, shrouds a copy of a bust of Beethoven by French sculptor Antoine Bourdelle.

ABOVE
Despite their 8-foot-tall height, Turk's-cap lilies are surprisingly delicate.

OPPOSITE
Dash added the postmodern Yellow Arch to the corridor between the Sunken Terrace and the Summer Studio in 1988. It echoes the arched doorway at the end of the path, which opens to the Summer House's guest bedroom. 'Casa Blanca' lilies grow to the left of the corridor.

BELOW
Underplanted with silver-leaved *Lamiastrum galeobdolon*, black hellebores stand out along the walkway.

RIGHT
To the east of the Yellow Arch and the corridor, a zigzag *Taxus* hedge is covered in burlap in the winter to prevent deer damage.

BELOW RIGHT
Snow clumps among the fragrant blooms of *Hamamelis* × *intermedia* 'Aurora', a witch hazel planted at the beginning of the path leading from the Summer Studio to the Sunken Terrace and Secret Garden.

Clematis virginiana comes into its own in early September outside the gravel-lined entrance to the Summer Studio. Dash commissioned a local ironmonger to make the chairs, copies of antique French originals that had rusted away.

CHAPTER FIFTEEN

The Secret Garden

By autumn, the Secret Garden is a lush paradise, anchored by towering red banana (*Ensete ventricosum* 'Maurelii') and *Colocasia gigantea.*

Aside from early plantings at the far edges of the property, intended as privacy screening and windbreaks, Madoo began in the Secret Garden, which Dash also called the Inner Garden. It didn't exist at all when he bought the fallow farmland.

While he was attending the University of New Mexico, Dash was likely influenced by adobe architecture and interior courtyards. Accordingly, the Summer House—comprising the original 1740 barn, the 1970s-era library, and the private quarters converted from nineteenth-century sheds—surrounds the Secret Garden on three sides, essentially forming a lush interior courtyard visible from eight of the Summer House's windows. It can be entered either from the house (private) or through the corridor connecting the Sunken Terrace to the Summer Studio (public).

For a time, the library's roof could be accessed via a staircase within the Secret Garden, positioned astride the Summer House's exterior. But a nonagenarian donor once climbed the rickety steps to take in the view and stood on the roof at great peril, as the surrounding balustrade had become wobbly and infirm. During the Summer House's 2015–16 restoration, the balustrade was replicated and the stairs removed altogether. The new, now inaccessible balustrade pays homage to Dash's inventiveness, but without the hazard and headache.

Dash made numerous paintings of the library and its roof, in addition to the sweeping vistas from on high. Oddly, many of these canvases feature a vase of flowers, as if the views—for a time, one could see the Atlantic Ocean—were not enough. The paintings provide a pictorial timeline of Madoo in its early stages, including plants that have come and gone and some that still thrive today. *Rosa* 'Dortmund', with its clear cerise petals, white eye, and golden boss of stamens, is among the latter, climbing a tall finial-topped post at the public entrance to the Secret Garden and even stretching into the branches of the Sunken Terrace's *Magnolia kobus*, if the gardeners don't get to it first. A repeat bloomer, 'Dortmund' is a cynosure, bright and attention-getting all summer long. A cutting taken from this venerable rose several years ago now blooms next to the door that provides access to the library and dining room.

The Secret Garden has undergone many iterations. Dash's taller-than-tall yellow hollyhocks thrived here for many years, heaps of manure at their feet. Early visitors to Madoo still remember them, and they are forever immortalized—in muddier tones—on a work on paper by Dash, who himself stood 6'2" and favored statuesque plants that grew into a veritable jungle by summer's end.

Several evergreens provide necessary year-round structure, including the last of the Irish junipers that used to proliferate at Madoo: It still manages to hold on. Every year, as in Dash's time, the juniper is cleaned of dead branches and detritus and tied up to make a giant blue-hued exclamation point in the Secret Garden's center, a purple clematis using it as a base on which to climb. Two hollies—one cloud-pruned and the other sheared into

MADOO SAGGAPONNACK N Y 11962

Close by the freshly clipped beehive holly is the fluffy, seriously generous Saint Bernard of a rose, the Chestnut rose [*Rosa roxburghii*], all a rose should be and rarely is. "I do hate you so," said Penelope Hobhouse. "I can't grow it."

--R. D.

OPPOSITE
The nineteenth-century wrought-iron gate to the Secret Garden is hung on a blue-painted wooden post. It holds back a ruffled moss rose, *Rosa roxburghii plena*, with vibrant pink blooms and ferny foliage (it's also known as the double chestnut rose, due to its bristle-covered buds and fruit). An Australian tree fern (*Dicksonia antarctica*), which spends its winters at a nearby greenhouse, enjoys the protected environment of the Secret Garden during most of the rest of the year.

a standard bell shape—add a fanciful note, although the cloud-pruned holly resembles a Smurf more than its elegant Japanese ideal. A Southern magnolia—Madoo can't get enough of this impressive tree—towers above the courtyard, perfuming the space with its heady scent in the summer ("The odor will make your head swim," Dash wrote) while dropping its giant seedpods on the library's roof with great big thuds in the autumn. It sheds its thick glossy leaves virtually everywhere.

A small pool that leaked was eventually gotten rid of, but Dash wanted a water feature, so he installed a stoup on a naïvely decorated concrete column situated outside the kitchen window. Fitted with a recirculating pump, the ersatz fountain's tiny pool is planted with papyrus and quietly burbles with a distinctly ecclesiastical air beneath a massive clump of ironweed, which is somewhat intimidating to look at until it unleashes its gorgeous deep purple flowers in late summer. The birds have happily taken to the stoup's siren call, anointing themselves every morning in the cool water.

During the Summer House's restoration, the Secret Garden's climbing hydrangea, jasmine, and roses were removed so that the building could be reshingled and doors and windows replaced. Even in such a small space, a sense of barrenness prevailed once the work was completed. A donor bestowed Madoo with a gift of three 6-foot-tall Australian tree ferns, which became the touchstone for a tropics-inspired transformation. Because they are not hardy, the trees are kept in plastic pots for easy transfer to a local greenhouse in the winter. The pots are rimmed with bamboo canes cut to size and studded with *Tillandsia*, tiny orchids, and *Tradescantia*.

Next to the dark green *Taxus* arch at the Secret Garden's public point of entry, a Tiffany lamp–like *Brugmansia* 'Ecuador Pink' spreads its almost foot-long trumpets of light peach–hued flowers and unleashes a gently fragrant scent in the evening. A stout birdbath, filled with a variety of ferns, sits between two glossy black-painted Victorian cast-iron chairs, which provide a lovely spot for admiring the garden's structure, edged in

LEFT
Victorian cast-iron chairs and a vintage birdbath planted with ferns have an exotic backdrop of *Crocosmia* 'Lucifer' and *Ensete ventricosum* 'Maurelii', a tropical banana that needs to be overwintered in Madoo's basement.

BELOW LEFT
The stoup fountain has a concrete column that is covered in moss by midsummer. Dwarf papyrus grows below.

BELOW
The planting beds in the Secret Garden are edged in 4-by-6-foot railway sleepers. The double-trunked holly is sheared yearly to maintain a shape sketched out by Dash twenty years ago.

MADOO SAGGAPONNACK N Y 11962

Pleasure-loving and sometimes dissolute popes as well as murderous Medicis and rich wannabes playing at being philosopher-farmers adored their secret gardens, enclosed green spaces with a bench or two, perhaps a fountain, a piece of marble sculpture, seldom any flowers, with a cypress or a bay for shade.

--R. D.

railway sleepers painted Madoo blue and lined with pots of succulents, somewhat reminiscent of the Jardin Majorelle in Marrakesh. The chairs lie within the shadow of a copper finial from the 1913 Cass Gilbert–designed neo-Gothic Woolworth Building in Manhattan, a gift from the late Beverley Galban. The impressive ornament rests atop a 5-foot-tall octagonal stand, lending a totemic aspect to the Secret Garden's meditative atmospherics.

Non-natives have now become de rigueur in this semishaded space. In Dash-planted beds of liriope, exotics now flourish, and these have decided flair: pointy-leaved *Veronicastrum* (it strips down to a terrific exoskeleton in the winter), *Lunaria annua* 'Chedglow' (bred by Rosemary Verey and pretty in pink), and even purple loosestrife, carefully managed to keep it in check. 'Lucifer', the tomato-red *Croscosmia*, attracts hummingbirds in summer. Additional plantings range from teasels (whose seed heads were once used to brush wool) to winter-blooming 'Carolina' jasmine and moss roses (*Rosa roxburghii*).

The liriope is ceding even more of its claim on the Secret Garden as we dig out chunks of the ubiquitous ground cover and pop in new perennials, including hardy arum lilies and *Hydrangea aspera* 'Plum Passion', a purple-leaved beauty that holds court in one corner. For the corner opposite, garden designer Timothy Heslop suggested a dramatic combination of hardy green banana (*Musa basjoo*) and 'Black Lace' elderberry (*Sambucus nigra*) plants. The Secret Garden's spiky acanthus blooms a bit later than it does on the slopes of the Acropolis, but it's no less impressive, and the red banana (*Ensete ventricosum* 'Maurelii'), which needs to spend bare-root winters in the basement, proudly unfurls its burgundy-stained leaves during its dramatic upward trajectory, a summertime spectacle that seemingly defies all odds.

A table accommodates just two in the idyllic Secret Garden, where sky-high ironweed (*Vernonia gigantea*) and Japanese hydrangea vine (*Schizophragma hydrangeoides*) nearly obscure the kitchen window.

OPPOSITE

Veronicastrum virginicum 'Fascination', a hardy perennial, lends further exotic appeal to the Secret Garden's plantings.

ABOVE

A variegated mayapple (*Podophyllum difforme*) and twinleaf (*Jeffersonia diphylla*) just below it grow in the shade outside the library door.

OPPOSITE
An original copper spire from the 1913 Woolworth Building was given to Madoo in 2017 by Dash's friend Beverley Galban and placed on a slightly flared, 4-foot-tall octagonal pedestal.

LEFT
Tubers for these dramatic *Colocasia gigantea* were given to Madoo by architect Michael Jones and fashion executive Fernando Rivera, a former Madoo Conservancy board member. They are at least three generations old.

BELOW
Dash's bedroom, as seen from the Secret Garden. Ferns and perennial begonias (*Begonia grandis*) grow below the window.

LEFT
Dried teasel seed heads are left in autumn as a source of food for birds.

ABOVE
Hardy pitcher plants (*Sarracenia* 'Martha's Furnace') are grown outside in a marble basin all year long. The container doesn't have a hole, so it makes for a perfect bog-like environment.

OPPOSITE
By late summer, it's often difficult to step into the Secret Garden via the library door, due to the dense planting scheme.

'Sheffield Pink' chrysanthemums bloom profusely from early October well into November.

Acknowledgments

The magical world that is Madoo would not have been possible if it weren't for the myriad people—the poets and artists and fellow gardeners, the neighbors and volunteers and casual acquaintances—who have passed through the garden's gates and left their indelible mark. The Madoo Conservancy was established as a nonprofit in 1994, and our deepest thanks are due to its founding board members who planted the proverbial seed: Donald J. Bruckmann, Ngaere Macray, William and Katharine Rayner, John Sargent, and Marco Polo Stufano. Newer board members and enthusiasts over the years have further nurtured our mission with their remarkable guidance and expertise and continue to do so to this day. We remain indebted to them, particularly longtime donors Ala and Ralph Isham, who were dear friends of Robert Dash and have been integral to maintaining his legacy.

Even the tiniest garden needs more than one set of hands to be fruitful. For more than twenty-five years, Carlos Hernandez and his crew, especially the astonishingly prescient plant-whisperer Julian Aristides Gonzalez, have pruned and cut and sheared and sown, carefully tending mere saplings till they have skyrocketed to astonishing heights. They have seen the garden grow more than anyone else.

From our first e-mail exchange with editor Makenna Goodman, it has been a pleasure to work with the talented and diligently focused team at Timber Press, including copyeditor Pam Kingsley, production editor Matthew Burnett, and designer Hillary Caudle, who took our scattered sketch of an idea and turned it into something beautiful, as any good gardener might do with a few seeds scratched into soil.

Our principal photographer, Tria Giovan, herself a longtime member and devoted supporter of the Madoo Conservancy, took the pictures that appear in this volume over the course of an entire year and then some. In sun and shadow, rain and snow ("Can you pop over to Madoo?" we'd text urgently. "The frost looks amazing on the witch hazel!"), she made a herculean effort to capture the seasonal whims and idiosyncrasies of the ever-mercurial Madoo. And although the garden is an undeniably wonderful place to get lost in, it doesn't hurt to have one's bearings, so our multitalented friend Thibaut De Coster graciously provided us with a sweet map to guide the way. Additionally, Charlotte Moss, Douglas Crase, Madison Cox, Marilee Foster, and Robert Storr penned thoughtful essays about the garden that they have come to love and admire, in very personal and different ways, and we thank them for their contributions.

A deeply talented and true visionary, Bob Dash left Madoo to us and to generations to come, something we can all be grateful for.

—A. S. and K. C.

Photo and Illustration Credits

Principal photography in this book is by Tria Giovan. Other photographers featured are as follows:

Karen Balogh, 13 (top)

Kendell Cronstrom, 177 (top), 210 (bottom left), 212

Robert Dash, 19 (bottom), 25 (top right), 32

Wendy Goodrich, 82 (top left)

Timothy Heslop, 13 (bottom left), 15 (right), 21, 146, 149, 164 (bottom)

Pingree Louchheim, 13 (bottom right)

Gary J. Mamay, 10, 11 (bottom), 12, 14, 18, 33 (bottom), 75, 135, 136, 151, 161 (top), 218, 219

Bärbel Miebach, 33 (top)

Meagan Ouderkirk, 8

Frank Polach, 73

John Reed, 11 (top)

Alejandro Saralegui, 41 (top left), 82 (bottom left), 173 (top left), 176, 194 (bottom), 197 (top right, bottom)

Page 4 map by Thibaut De Coster

Index

--S

PHOTO BY GEORGIA OETKER

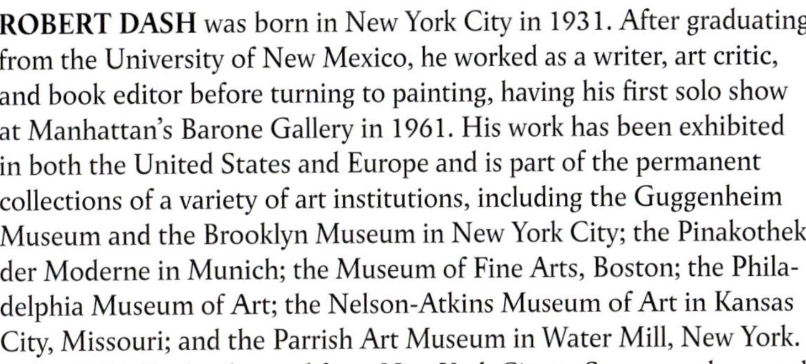

ROBERT DASH was born in New York City in 1931. After graduating from the University of New Mexico, he worked as a writer, art critic, and book editor before turning to painting, having his first solo show at Manhattan's Barone Gallery in 1961. His work has been exhibited in both the United States and Europe and is part of the permanent collections of a variety of art institutions, including the Guggenheim Museum and the Brooklyn Museum in New York City; the Pinakothek der Moderne in Munich; the Museum of Fine Arts, Boston; the Philadelphia Museum of Art; the Nelson-Atkins Museum of Art in Kansas City, Missouri; and the Parrish Art Museum in Water Mill, New York.

In 1967, Dash relocated from New York City to Sagaponack, a small hamlet on the East End of Long Island, to the home and garden he christened Madoo. Here, he painted, wrote poetry, and gardened for the rest of his life. In 1994, Madoo became a nonprofit public garden, and in 2011, Dash's archive of poetry and garden writings was acquired by Yale University's Beinecke Rare Book & Manuscript Library. Dash died at Madoo in 2013.

PHOTO BY CARL TIMPONE/BFA.COM

ALEJANDRO SARALEGUI was born and raised in Bronxville, New York. He started his career at the Metropolitan Museum of Art after receiving an undergraduate degree in art history from SUNY Purchase. He worked for art galleries, magazines, and fashion and gardening companies before becoming the executive director of the Madoo Conservancy in 2009. He lives in Bridgehampton, New York.

PHOTO BY CARL TIMPONE/BFA.COM

KENDELL CRONSTROM, a native of Minneapolis, attended Cornell University and the University of Minnesota, where he graduated with a degree in journalism. A longtime magazine editor, he has worked at a host of publications ranging from *Vanity Fair* to *Elle Decor* and was the editor in chief of *Hamptons Cottages & Gardens* for fourteen years. Currently the vice president of marketing for Schumacher, he lives in Brooklyn and Bridgehampton, New York.

Frontispiece: In spring, magnolia petals fill the Sunken Terrace, as tulips emerge from the double pot in the foreground.

Photo and illustration credits appear on page 255.

Timber Press
Workman Publishing
Hachette Book Group, Inc.
1290 Avenue of the Americas
New York, New York 10104
timberpress.com

Timber Press is an imprint of Workman Publishing, a division of Hachette Book Group, Inc. The Timber Press name and logo are registered trademarks of Hachette Book Group, Inc.

Printed in Dongguan, China (TLF), on responsibly sourced paper

Text and cover design by Hillary Caudle

ISBN 978-1-64326-419-6
A catalog record for this book is available from the Library of Congress.